The Modfather

My Life With Paul Weller

David Lines

arrow books

Published by Arrow Books 2007

5 7 9 10 8 6 4

This book is a work of non-fiction based on the life, experiences and recollections of the author. In some limited cases names of people, places, dates, sequences or the detail of events have been changed solely to protect the privacy of others. The author has warranted to the publishers that, except in such minor respects not affecting the substantial accuracy of the work, the contents of this book are true. Whilst the publishers have taken care to explore and check where reasonably possible, they have not verified all the information in this book and do not warrant its veracity in all respects.

First published in Great Britain in 2006 by William Heinemann

Arrow Books
The Random House Group Limited
20 Vauxhall Bridge Road, London SW1V 2SA

www.randomhouse.co.uk

Addresses for companies within The Random House Group Limited can be found at:
www.randomhouse.co.uk/offices.htm

The Random House Group Limited Reg. No. 954009

A CIP catalogue record for this book
is available from the British Library

ISBN 9780099476597

The Random House Group Limited supports The Forest Stewardship Council (FSC), the leading international forest certification organisation. All our titles that are printed on Greenpeace approved FSC certified paper carry the FSC logo. Our paper procurement policy can be found at:
www.rbooks.co.uk/environment

Typeset in Perpetua by
Palimpsest Book Production Limited, Grangemouth, Stirlingshire
Printed in the UK by CPI Bookmarque, Croydon, CR0 4TD

The Modfather

David Lines was born in Nottingham in 1967. He has written for radio, stage and various newspapers and magazines. He lives in Yorkshire with his wife and two daughters.

Praise for *The Modfather*

'I never much liked Paul Weller's music, but David Lines' book convinced me I was wrong – his teenage obsession with The Jam, and Paul Weller in particular, was so infectious I decided I'd missed something. I actually went out and bought a couple of The Jam's albums and re-listened to them pretending I was a teenage David Lines. Doing that, I found I rather liked them. When I listened again as me, I didn't. It was the teenage David Lines that had got under my skin. He's a great explainer of pop music and what it means to young people. Every marketing man at every record company should read this book.' Simon Napier-Bell, author of *Black Vinyl White Powder*

'Introducing the Adrian Mole of mod . . . a charming book packed with musical nostalgia, embarrassing misadventures and formative drinking experiences. Fans of Andrew Collins and Nick Hornby would approve.' *Q*

'Equal parts *High Fidelity*, *The King of Comedy* and *The Catcher in the Rye*, Lines' *The Modfather* is a very readable tale of fandom that fizzes with nail-biting obsession, heartbreak and ear-ticklingly funny misunderstandings.' *Mojo*

'An engaging portrait of a Mod-man Billy Liar for whom Weller's songs served as the narrative thread holding together his teenage dreams and ambitions' *Metro*

'The story is solid and innocently told with an equal measure of humour and sadness . . . Even if you're not a Weller fan, this book is well worth a read' *Record Collector*

'A solid chuck of pure passion.' *Ladsmag – Sunday Sport*

For my Father

Acknowledgements

Heartfelt thanks to
Susan Sandon, Justine Taylor and Ann Evans

Looking back now, I don't know what exactly it was that I was looking for, or indeed if I was looking for anything. What I do know, is that when I discovered The Jam, they changed my life forever. At the time, it seemed that before them there was nothing and once I'd found them – there was everything. Listening to Paul, Bruce and Rick was like unlocking a great, big door, opening it up and stepping out into the most glorious, blazing sunshine.

What I didn't realise was just how much my life would come to revolve around The Jam and how, overnight, it seemed my fixation with Paul Weller came to dominate my teenage years and could – at best – be described as unhealthy and at worst, obsessive. This is my story, it's about my friends and my family, my haircuts, shampoo and shoes, music and modernism. It's all about how I grew up with Paul Weller. This was my modern world – and you're most welcome to join me in it.

1

When I'm Young

Saturday mornings were when it normally happened, I'd say about once every three or four weeks on average. I realise now it was an act of great love, although it didn't feel like one at the time. When I was very little, I didn't mind it at all, in fact I quite enjoyed it, but once I had turned ten and started to find myself becoming more conscious of the way I looked, it slowly became something I dreaded. I would carry a kitchen stool up the staircase, behind my father, as we made our way to the bathroom and I'd set it down on the floor, hop on and tightly shut my eyes. A cigarette burned in the ashtray on the windowsill and on the shelf next to it was a domestic collection of the tools of his trade, smaller and less extensive than those which were at the shop, but nevertheless impressive: a cut-throat razor, scissors, water spray, combs and a talcum-powder puffer which made a noise like a sigh when you squeezed it. I would sit as still as a statue until Dad's work was done. 'There you are, lad – a perfect short back and sides . . .'

Once Dad stopped working Saturdays, that's when he cut my hair. For years he worked with his dad, my Grampa Lines, in the family barber's shop on The Avenue in West Bridgford, a leafy suburb of Nottingham. I was born on 15 February, 1967 (I've always regretted missing Valentine's Day by a whisker). Mum had decided that with us three boys, that's me and younger brothers Chris, aged seven, and Phil, five, it was high time Dad got a proper job, not just one where he got paid out of the till at the end of each day. So, after ten years, Dad left the family business and went to work as a sales rep for Pompadour, the hair care wholesaler, where he sold things like coconut oil shampoo and condoms, disposable razors, Brylcreem and Cossack hairspray which came in bright red aerosol cans with a fierce Russian horseman on the front. He sold this stuff to Grampa, who never really forgave him for going. Mum would ask, 'Did you see your father today?'

'Yes, Margaret, I did.'

'And did he buy much stock from you?'

'Now that you come to mention it, no.'

My father's name was Bill Lines and he was without doubt a sharp-dressed man. Six foot tall, slim, broad shoulders, olive skin, mohair suit and perfect, dark brown hair. He wore it short, with a side parting, shaved close into the nape of his neck and he was never without a Players Navy Cut on the go. He became a barber because his father was a barber. And his father became a barber because his father left him, as a baby, on the steps of a barber's shop. The Pughs had no children of their own and they took him in, adopted him and raised him as their own. From the age of nine, he worked in the barber's shop all the hours that God sent and when they died, they left it to him. At twenty-six he was his own businessman and Dad used to say that he wished it was that easy for all of us, but I never knew what he meant. I used to think that it couldn't have been that easy for Grampa Lines, I mean, not knowing who your real parents were couldn't have been that easy.

It wasn't until years later that I discovered why Grampa used to let Slack Alice live in his loft. It turned out that she was a distant Pugh and Grampa felt as if he owed her a roof. She was mad, and ate chocolate cake all day long.

I used to walk past her door and there she was, through the crack in it, like something out of Hinge and Bracket. 'Come inside, I've got a *slice* . . .' One year she was arrested in the park for taking off all of her clothes and carting a young boy away under her arm. She went to hospital for a week and when she came back we were told never to mention it again. The day they let her out and she went back to Grampa and Granny's I took a Lyon's chocolate sponge cake up to her room, knocked and put it on the plate outside her door. 'There's cake outside if you want it.' An hour later it was still there, completely untouched. Dad said she'd have leapt on it before she'd had her treatment. 'Must have put an extra fifty pence in the meter and cranked the thing right up before they wired it up to her.'

Dad told me about the one day that Slack Alice

worked in the shop. Grampa asked her to add up some cheques. Fifteen minutes later he went into the tea room where she was and found her struggling to count on her fingers.

'Have you added up those cheques yet?'

'I think so.'

'And?'

'There's four of them.'

In the evenings Dad sold insurance, riding around Bridgford on his scooter, seeing his clients and selling them policies. Occasionally he'd also drive cabs for Brown's Bridgford Taxis, going straight from insurance on the scooter to cabbying in the car, and would work late through the night till the early morning light. The only way I could hear him before I went to sleep was for me to tune the radio to the short wave and listen out amongst the police band and the Gas Board.

'Forty-two, forty-two, come in forty-two. You've got a wait and return from number eleven Pierpoint Road. Roger that, forty-two?'

A crackle of radio static, then 'Forty-two here. Roger that, base.'

Underneath my covers I'd shine the torch close up to the speaker and whisper into it.

'Goodnight, Dad. Drive safely and remember – I love you. Roger that?'

Bedtime became fun when Dad wasn't there at night, I used to get such a thrill out of secretly listening to him, picturing where he was going, imagining who he'd picked up. The next morning I'd play little games with him, never once letting on.

'Did you pick up anyone famous last night?'

'I did – Brian Clough. Had to pour him out of the pub – anyway, how did you know?'

'I didn't. Just asking . . .'

Mum was ten years younger than Dad. She played Beatles records and smoked cigarettes on the top decks of buses; she painted her toenails in the garden, then stretched out on the sunlounger. She had beautiful Titian hair and sang songs when she was sewing or baking a cake. Uncle Nick (Mum's big brother) and Auntie Gill, plus cousins Zoe and Kirsty lived in Bridgford too.

Mum and Dad first met at the local tennis court and three months later, when she finally introduced him to her parents, Dad came face to face with a man whose hair he'd been cutting for the past eight years and who always bought 'something for the weekend' from him.

Apparently he never did again. Thinking about it now, I'd hate to think that meeting my father put an end to Granny and Grampa Sewter's sex life.

One day Dad's scooter went kaput. Because we didn't have a car, this was a serious crisis, as it meant that his evening insurance job would be on hold till a replacement was found. It was simple really – with no transport, there was less money coming in. That week's copy of *Exchange and Mart* came up trumps – there was a scooter advertised. Dad went to look at it and he liked it so much he bought it on the spot and rode it home. It was a very different sort of scooter, a Lambretta, and I was in awe of its grace and beauty. White, with a calfskin seat, three sets of chrome mirrors and a chrome rack on the back as well as red, white and blue tassels which hung from the handlebar grips. Whoever owned it before had loved it very much.

'The chap I bought it off was at great pains to tell me it's a scooter and not a moped, he made himself very clear about that.'

Mum winked at Dad and said, 'Very nice. Are you planning on riding down to Brighton at the weekend?' He didn't seem to understand. 'Brighton? No, but I am thinking about going up to Leeds sometime soon.'

Mum raised an eyebrow and asked why.

'Nothing for you to worry about . . .'

We put it down to his job with Pompadour and left it at that. Dad kick-started his scooter and the thing purred, not like his old one which sort of coughed-up phlegm before it got going, and Dad set off. I ran down the drive and watched him scooter away into the distance. He looked like a god on that thing.

The next day I went straight to the local bike shop. Oil and rubber filled the air, and I had the contents of my piggy bank in my hot little fist. The last time I was there was in the autumn when Dad brought me in to buy a new saddlebag to keep conkers in. The same man who sold us the saddlebag appeared.

'Can I help you, son?'

'How many chrome mirrors can I buy with six pounds and fifteen pence?'

It turned out that I could buy four mirrors, which was two sets, a whippy aerial and a roll of black and white chequered sticky tape exactly the same as on Dad's scooter. I pedalled home as fast as I could, fitted the mirrors and the aerial and stuck tape on the front forks and then I looked just like my dad.

* * *

On Thursday nights I'd cling for dear life to Dad. I'd be on the back of the Lambretta and we'd zoom our way round to Grampa Lines. It was the same every Thursday, Spot the Ball night. Dad and Grampa would sit hunched over the grainy, black and white picture in the *Evening Post*. Grampa would get his massive magnifying glass out and Granny Lines would busy herself in the tiny kitchen, warming her pot. Dad and Grampa had been trying to guess where the football was every Thursday night since before I was born.

Suddenly, Grampa threw back his head and leaned in with the glass. He looked just like Sherlock Holmes. 'Bill, look closely – I think we may very well have found it . . .'

'Where?'

'There. Above that bloke's bobble hat in the second row. Next to that troublemaker with the long hair. Needs a damn good short back and sides.'

Dad said, 'The one who looks like Barry Sheene?'

'If you say so. Him, anyway.' Grampa circled the spot with a thin finger.

We never did win. Dad opened that paper every Saturday and always said the same thing.

'Bugger. That was a close one, that was. We were just a hair's breadth out . . .'

The week that Granny Lines died we all cried buckets. She was lovely, and I knew that she was poorly but I didn't know she was that poorly. I used to help her sweep up the hair in the shop and she was always telling me not to open the sterilising cabinet. 'Don't look inside there – you'll go blind.'

Dad took Chris, Phil and I to see her the Saturday before she died. Granny was in bed, propped up on pillows with her silver hair held back off her bony face with clips. An oak ashtray shaped like an enormous chess piece stood by the side of the bed and Granny was as white as the Senior Service pinched between her lips, and probably just as thin. She reached inside her handbag, took out her purse and threw three fifty-pence pieces at us. They didn't get far, not past the end of the bed. Dad plucked them from the camberwick bedspread and handed us one each.

'Bill, make sure they buy something nice, won't you. Let the boys get themselves some sweets. They like sweets, don't they?'

'Yes, Mum. They like sweets. Say thank you to Granny, you three.'

We did, and Chris and Phil raced off to the newsagent's on the corner and came back ten minutes later with paper bags full of Refreshers and Cola Bottles, CurlyWurlys and red liquorice laces. I didn't, I was saving my money for different laces which would come in a pair of suede shoes, just like Dad's.

We never saw Granny again. But we did see her handbag, because Grampa had taken to carrying the thing around with him all day long. I loved Grampa, but I didn't love him nearly as much when he started carting dead Granny's handbag everywhere. It was incredibly embarrassing. He took his lunch to the shop in it, the takings to the bank in it and at the end of each day he bought a bottle of Scotch and took that home in it too. I knew this because I'd heard Mum and Dad talking about it one morning when I was getting ready for school.

'Bill, you've got to talk to him about his drinking. Your father's going to the shop half-pissed every morning – if he's not careful he'll have some poor sod's ear off . . .'

* * *

It was the Queen's Silver Jubilee. I was excited because we'd been doing a project about it at school when they announced on the news that the Queen was coming to visit West Bridgford. I told Mum that I didn't know that where we lived was so important, and she told me that it wasn't and that the Queen was visiting everywhere in the country and anyway, she'd have to meet Brian Clough so maybe she wouldn't come after all.

It was the day of the street party and, even though it was a Friday, we were all in our Sunday best. Everyone from Selby Road was there, as well as some characters I'd never seen before. They had brightly coloured hair, pink, blue and green which stood up in huge spikes on top whilst the rest of their heads were shaved bald. They wore safety pins through their noses and had menacing-looking chains which hung from their trousers. They drank beer out of cans and to me – and everyone else – they may as well have come from another planet. One of them had painted 'God save the Queen' on the back of her biker jacket. Irony had yet to enter my orbit, and I'd never even heard of The Sex Pistols. These punks looked frightening to me, but they had something about them which I liked, some sort of bravado, some sort of style.

Grampa Lines was right next to them, eating a piece of flapjack and carrying his handbag. He was just standing there, two feet away, just staring at them like animals in a cage at the zoo. I got the feeling that they might turn at any minute.

'Mum, who are those people and what are they doing here?'

'Which people?'

'Those people. The ones over there.' Mum told me not to point because it was rude.

'Oh, you mean the dodgy ones with the funny coloured hair?'

'Yes, the ones with the hair.'

Mum knelt down and whispered in my ear. 'The one with the purple rinse is Mrs Gregg and the one with the bright blue hair is her sister. Don't worry, I can't see them causing any trouble – they haven't got a single hip between them.'

Grampa Lines sidled over looking all handbag and disgusted. 'I've never seen anything so disgraceful. Have you seen the state of their hair? There should be a law against it.'

Mum winked at me and Grampa went on. 'It shouldn't be allowed, it's upsetting to look at and it's disrespectful to the Queen. I've a good mind to go and say something, go and give them a piece of my mind.'

I said, 'I know, what with it being the Jubilee you'd have thought she'd have kept her hair silver instead of dyeing it blue.'

Grampa was not impressed. 'Don't be disrespectful to your elders – Mrs Gregg's husband lost both his feet last week.'

That shut me up, but only for a minute. 'Really, Grampa? I didn't know that they came off.'

He gave me a quick clip round the ear and as I winced and turned my head I saw Dad running down the street towards us at breakneck speed. I remember thinking what a weird sight that was. I'd never seen him running before and, thinking about it now, I don't think that I ever saw him doing it again. He wasn't the sort to get involved in that sort of thing.

Dad ran like mad and waved at the same time and when he got to us he was almost completely out of breath. He smoothed down his hair and gave Mum a peck on the cheek. 'Where's Chris and Phil?'

'Granny Sewter's taken them to throw wet sponges at the vicar.'

'They'll like that – but not as much as he will.'

Grampa Lines scuttled over to Dad. 'I was just saying, Bill, I was just saying, it's absurd the way those louts look, it's not attractive to look at. There must be something wrong inside their minds. What kind of healthy mind walks around looking like that?' This, coming from a man carrying a lady's handbag full of flapjack.

Mum rolled her eyes and Dad smiled back, weakly.

Grampa found another high horse and got back on. 'If the police are allowing animals like that lot to roam the streets of Bridgford, God alone knows what they're getting up to in the inner cities.'

Dad went a slightly yellow colour and suddenly found his cufflinks fascinating.

'Eh, Bill? I say, if they're like this here now, what's going on elsewhere?'

Dad lit a cigarette and ran his hand through his hair. He looked scared. 'I'll let you know, Dad. We're moving to Leeds.' Behind his head the bunting fluttered, all red, white and blue and deep in my stomach a thousand butterflies broke free.

That trip to Leeds which Dad had mentioned wasn't to sell shaving foam: it was for an interview. He'd got the job as a sales rep for AMF Clarbro, a company which made machines for the clothing industry. Our lives were going to be turned upside down. But not for almost eight months: Dad had to complete three months' probation, then there was a delay to his start date because the person he was replacing was staying on longer before he left, and then there was the task of finding our new house. By the time we were ready to go I was eleven, and had started 'big school' at West Bridgford Comprehensive. I fitted in well, liked the teachers and my new fellow pupils. I did not want to go.

We were in the kitchen. Chris, Phil, Mum and Dad and I were all scrunched up around the Formica table. Tea was finished and the plates cleared off the table and replaced by an AA road map of Great Britain. Dad took the top off a red biro and drew a small circle. He prodded a dot in the centre of it and said, 'Right, that's where we are now.'

Chris sucked thoughtfully on a banana and toffee Chuppa Chup – he was rarely seen without one. He gave it a lick and asked, 'And where are we going to, Dad?'

Dad turned two pages and hunted around for a bit then drew another circle. 'There,' he said.

At the time, it felt flicking through those two pages was like flying across continents. The distance between here and there looked like a lifetime, and little Phil started crying. Chris stuck his lolly in Phil's mouth and it did the trick. All of a sudden I felt consumed by fear. 'But Dad, where *is* Leeds?' I whined.

Dad lit a Players and jabbed again at the map. 'It's here, lad. In Yorkshire,' and he blew smoke towards the open back door.

'Will we need passports? Yorkshire's not in Nottingham, is it?' Chris asked.

I could tell this wasn't going as well as Dad planned. He answered, trying to stay calm, 'No, we'll only need passports if we were going abroad, leaving the country. And we're not leaving the country, we're only going an hour and a half up the bloody road.'

I was not convinced, and asked, 'Which road?'

Mum straightened her skirt and lit one of Dad's fags. She flicked her hair back and picked mascara from the corner of one eye before trying to put us at ease. 'The M1. Look, kids – your Dad and I have talked this thing through till we're blue in the face and we know we're doing this for the best. Your Dad's got a great new job, a smart new car and we can live in a bigger house. We're moving on, and it'll be fun. Believe me.'

I didn't believe her and my head span at the thought. 'I don't like Yorkshire pudding,' I said, then asked, 'What will happen to Grampa Lines?'

Mum shot back with 'He'll be all right – he's got his Scotch,' and right away, by the look on Dad's face I could see just how much she regretted saying it. I helped set the table for dessert, and after about ten minutes Mum had another try at helping Dad convince us. 'Your Dad's somehow – and don't ask me how – managed to make a great chance for us all and we'd be daft as brushes not to take it. I know that moving away's a hard thing to do, but we've just got to grin and bear it. It'll mean he can swap his scooter for a real Austin Maxi and, frankly, that's good enough for me. There's even talk of a tow bar . . .'

I couldn't help repeating what Grampa Lines had been saying about Leeds. 'Good. We'll need it up there to help bring in the coal.'

Mum's lips tightened. 'Don't you go listening to your Grampa Lines. It's not all pits and ponies up there, you know. I even read that Leeds city centre's getting its own Chelsea Girl.'

'But I'm a boy,' I protested.

'That's not what I mean, David, and you know it. Leeds isn't the end of the world, not by a long chalk.' So that was it. We were moving to Leeds. Dad spent the next three months working up there at the head office and the four of us prepared ourselves for the jolt. I almost gave up listening to the police band on the radio what with Dad no longer cabbying at night, but the exciting bug of eavesdropping had burrowed too far underneath my skin ever to leave, and to this day I still get a thrill from overhearing a secret snippet on someone's shortwave.

I can remember when Dad brought home a photograph of the house. It was the first time any of us had seen what it was like. Mum said that it was nice knowing where we were going to be living. From her tone I knew that she'd have liked for us all to have gone and seen it before Dad bought it.

Mum was in the kitchen and I'd just got home from school. It was my last week as we were due to move on Saturday. 'Mum, I need to ask you something.'

She stopped whisking up Angel Delight and switched Kate Bush off the radio. 'What's up, soldier?'

'It's something I've heard about Dad. Something Ralph Steele said about him.'

There was a look on her face and she didn't like the way this was going; maybe it was my imagination playing tricks on me, maybe it was nothing. 'What? What have you heard?'

'Ralph Steele said that Dad is a mod because the scooter has mirrors all over it and he said that his dad says that all mods are bum boys. Mum, what's a mod? And what's a bum boy?'

I could sense Mum's relief when my question turned out to be something silly, and she smiled to herself and switched the radio back on. 'I've got no idea what a bum boy is, darling. And your father rides a scooter because he does, he just does. He used to be a barber, that's why he's got a smart haircut and he's always liked to wear a decent suit. That doesn't necessarily mean that he has to ride to the seaside at weekends and hit strangers over the head with a deckchair. Understand?'

'Not really, Mum, no. Do they have mods and bum boys in Leeds?'

'I have no idea. And anyway, now your Dad's got the company car he won't need the scooter – he's selling it to the bloke taking over his insurance run. Now, go and clean your rabbit hutch out, there's a good boy.'

We moved up to Leeds five days later. Ninety-three Fairburn Drive was our new home. It was a three-bedroomed detached house, on a corner with a low wall all the way round. Behind that was the second line of defence, a row of conifers no higher than three feet. The house had a slightly larger garden than the old one, and the front of it was pink pebble-dash. There was a nice front garden, too, with roses and neatly kept beds. Inside, it was like the house in Bridgford, except where there had been a sitting room, there was now a lounge that led through to the dining room, and beyond that, French windows which opened onto a small patio and the lawn. I liked it. Across the road from us were three large, square grassed areas. I watched the local kids playing football on them and wondered when I'd summon up courage to get to know them all. I had a single bedroom to myself at the front of the house, and Chris and Phil shared a bunk bed in the double room at the back of the house. Ours was the nicest looking one on the estate, which must have been built in the sixties.

* * *

In Bridgford, the house which we left behind was a quarter of the way up a road a mile long. The higher up you went, the bigger and more stately the houses became. At the very top of Selby Road the houses were like mansions, with massive iron gates; one even had a pool. Despite us being near the bottom of the road it was still a lovely place to grow up. It had a warmth, a kindness to it, and if it sounds like I'm peering back through the kaleidoscope of nostalgia – I'm not. West Bridgford was homely and Garforth was an alien landscape. Garforth had council estates not far from ours, where windows were replaced by boards and it was intimidating even to walk past them sometimes. The people were different there. They looked different and they sounded different and all I wanted was to be back in Bridgford. That wasn't going to happen – I just had to get on with it.

New School. Never have two words struck such fear into the heart of an impressionable and sensitive eleven-year-old boy. Especially when that new school was almost a hundred miles away in some strange and distant land called Yorkshire. Garforth Comprehensive looked like a prison. To be more precise, it looked like the H-block. A cold hard slab of institutionalised concrete surrounded by acres of warm, green playing fields, the school appeared to me like an almighty visiting spaceship which had simply landed in the middle of a field. Only once inside, I was the alien. To the front of it was the concrete playground, accessed by sets of steps from each of its four corners. It was ten feet below the level of the rest of the school and was affectionately referred to as 'The Sunken'.

The first lesson I had was rugby. I'd had to sit an assessment exam which took half the morning, then was taken down to meet my new form who were doing sports. As I'd not been given a timetable I didn't know that it was a sports day, so one of the secretaries took me to the changing rooms and told me to wait there till the end of that period when I could meet my new classmates. As I stepped inside, what I saw chilled me to the marrow.

Inside, lined up beneath the jumpers, shirts and trousers that hung messily on pegs, were maybe thirty pairs of the most terrifying footwear I had ever seen. Great, menacing boots of varying sizes, some black and some cherry red, some with red laces, some with black laces and yet all of the same design, all with evil black labels sticking out the top with a bright yellow, vivid electric typeface, like lightning bolts, proclaiming two words: Air Wair.

I seriously thought that my new class must have been playing an away team from the local barracks. Surely only a squadron of soldiers would wear these things on their feet? Dear God, if these were my classmates' boots then they must be the hardest people on the planet. I stepped outside, and through the rolling mist over the distant playing fields watched my new form literally kicking seven shades out of each other. Welcome to your new school, David.

I envied Chris and Phil having new friends come home to our house for tea. They both went to Green Lane Junior School, just up the road from the house, and weren't yet of an age where tribalism and what you wore on your feet determined who'd be your mate. They were still playing games like cowboys and indians and I wished then that I was as well. It's a very thin line between being a child and being eleven. Everything seemed so much simpler for them. In contrast, things at my school were steadily becoming unbearable. I wasn't being picked on, I wasn't making any enemies, I just wasn't being anything, really. Looking back, if I was anything I was lost. It didn't help being invisible. I was entirely invisible and that was because it was the easiest thing to be. Despite this, it just wasn't me. I didn't feel comfortable not being seen.

It was Sunday, a family day out in Dad's new company car. We'd got a chocolate brown Austin Maxi 1750 HLS complete with tartan rug on the parcel shelf, and yes, the tow bar was there, too. We were going to Scarborough for the first time for a walk along the big beach and cliffs and have fish and chips and eat them on the front. Dad took his binoculars because he loved looking at the ships out at sea. We were stuck in a traffic jam on the A64 and had moved maybe six feet in half an hour. Chris and Phil were busy wriggling around, playing I spy and getting bored, just like me. I started to daydream and from nowhere, whilst I stared up at the cloudless sky, there came a distant buzzing which very quickly grew louder. It sounded like we were suddenly going to be overtaken by a swarm of mechanical honey bees. I turned and looked out of the back window, back down the dual carriageway as the road surface shimmered in the sun, and there, right there, was the most impressive sight I had ever seen in my entire life. An army was coming, an invasion in a sea of green. Wave after wave of bright, shiny scooters buzzed towards us, weaving in and out of the traffic, engulfing the car. I was dazzled by the gracious necks of the machines, so fluid and birdlike, like a huge flock of chrome swans. I felt as if they had come to rescue me.

The riders had badges and beer towels sewn onto their coats and a few of them had the words 'The Jam' spray-painted onto the back of them. I asked Dad what it meant and he said that he didn't know, but we were stuck in a traffic jam then. He also told me that those glittering riders were mods, and it was then that I knew that I wanted to be part of them, part of their gang with their white socks flashing above bright, shiny shoes and desert boots just like Dad's.

I tried to count them all as they washed over us and I got to a hundred and then lost count. The desire to get out of the car and climb onto the back of one of those scooters and be taken off somewhere magical was overwhelming. Without so much as a second thought I opened the door, in a trance, and I put one foot out onto the motorway, and before I knew it, Dad screamed and shouted at me to get back inside the car before I got run over. I did, and Chris and Phil laughed at me and Mum told me not to be such an idiot. Dad gave me the silent treatment. Once calm was restored, Mum asked me what possessed me to try and get out. I made an excuse about needing a pee. I thought it did the trick, but my brothers taunted me for the rest of the day. 'David wants a wee, David wants a wee,' they sang all the way there and then all the way home. I didn't mind, all I cared about was becoming part of that gang of mods.

What I didn't know then was that it wasn't a gang – it was a way of life.

'Why don't you join a club?' Mum had come back from the library. 'Meet some new people that way. I was putting my name down for *The Thorn Birds* and saw lots of clubs and societies up on the notice board.'

'Er, like what, exactly?'

'Like a photography club, like a stamp-collecting club, like a cycling club, like a birdwatching club, there's a chess club and a rambling club and all sorts of clubs for all sorts of people. I might even join one myself.'

'Why?' Mum didn't strike me as the sort of person to join a club.

'So I might meet someone to talk to. You're not the

only one who gets lonely, you know.' Mum lit a cigarette and disappeared into the garden with a cup of coffee.

I went to the library on my bike the next day. It was nice inside, with a shiny floor that squeaked when you walked across it and as many books as I could ever imagine. If I sat down then and started to read them all, I'd be dead before I finished even half of them. I immediately felt at home. We liked books in our house, I almost always got them as presents at birthdays and Christmas. Dad liked biographies and Mum read romantic fiction. I wasn't there for books, though. I was there to join their record library.

I signed up and got three orange tickets. This meant I could get three albums for three weeks each. I spent hours trying to decide which ones to get and finally came up with my three choices. They were: The Beatles – *Rubber Soul* (I chose this because Mum liked them); second choice was *Grease – The Album* (everyone else seemed to like it so I decided to give it a try and see if I did, too); my third choice was *This Is The Modern World*, by a band called The Jam, and I chose it because I remembered seeing their name written on the back of one of the scooterists when we went to the seaside.

There was another album by The Jam, called *In The City*, but it was on loan so I put my name down and the girl behind the desk said it'd be back next week.

I never even listened to *Grease* and although I liked *Rubber Soul*, it was The Jam for me. When I put those twelve inches of black vinyl on the record player in the living room, it was like throwing open a window and breathing in a whole new life.

There are some incredible songs on this album. My favourite was 'The Modern World' and it sounded like a gun going off inside my head. There were three people in The Jam: Paul Weller, who wrote most of the lyrics, played lead guitar and sang; Bruce Foxton, who also wrote two songs on this record, and played bass guitar; and then there was Rick Buckler, who was the drummer. When Paul Weller sang the words to 'The Modern World', he didn't so much sing them as cough them up and spit them into my face. It was like getting washed in someone else's anger – and I loved it. I loved the second song, 'London Traffic', less, but the third track, 'Standards', was as bitter and urgent as a bullet. In it, Paul warned against what would happen to us if we didn't conform – he sang, 'You know what happened to Winston' and I went and asked Mum about what happened to Churchill. It was years later that I found, much to my shame, that Paul was referring to Winston Smith from Orwell's *Nineteen Eighty-Four*.

'Standards' was actually written about Weller's horror at The Sex Pistols being dropped by their record company just because some Conservative Member of Parliament told them to. It's amusing to me now, but back then I thought he was telling me not to hand in my homework on time. It's funny how everything he wrote seemed so personal. It's even funnier today, when it all still does. What I love about this album is how one minute it sounds as insistent as an ambulance and the next as tender as a whisper in your ear.

When I'd listened to *In The City*, my made was mind up – The Jam were my band.I could see and hear what Paul was doing with these records. Despite hearing the second album before the first, or because of it, I could sense similarities, such as the way both albums open with the most blistering and powerful song on each record. You'd expect the albums to go downhill from thereon, but they don't, they build on each opening track. The opening songs are statements, more than anything, they set you up for the rest of each record, although nothing could have set me up for the

Batman theme on 'In The City'. Some of the songs on this first album sounded to me like speeded-up rock and roll and I wasn't as keen as I was with *This Is The Modern World*. 'Away From The Numbers', though, on *In The City*, immediately became my fave song of all time ever, and even though it's about a mod stepping outside of his clan and taking a look at his world and that of the world around him and needing to take a break from it, I didn't know this, and interpreted it as a sympathetic ear to how poor I was at arithmetic, and copied the lyrics down on the inside cover of my maths book.

All of my school workbooks were instantly re-covered with pictures of The Jam which I cut out of *Sounds* and the *NME*. My English exercise book had a picture of Paul on the front. In it, he looked pensive and slightly sullen. My geography book had a picture of Paul on it – in it he looked sullen and slightly pensive. General science had a picture of all of The Jam on. In it, they all looked rather moody. The navy blue haversack which I carried them to and from school in became adorned with the spray-painted logo that The Jam used, although I didn't use an aerosol can like they did, I used a black marker pen and went over and over it till the ink ran out. It looked brilliant. Until it rained, and then it just looked crap, like it was crying.

Finally things were picking up for me – it felt like me and my three brilliant new friends, Paul, Bruce and Rick, had known each other forever. We were as thick as thieves, we were going to stick together for the rest of our lives. Sure, they were older than me, but that didn't matter at all. They talked to me in the most honest, open and passionate way, through their songs, through their music and through the interviews and articles which I hunted down each week in *Sounds* and the *NME*. I cut out interviews and stuck them to my bedroom wall. Sometimes, I bought two copies – one for my wall and one for my scrapbooks.

Paul especially knew what it was like to be me, he knew that we were worlds apart from everyone else. We shared the sense that something was not quite right between us and the rest of the world and listening to Paul's take on this made life in a new school so much easier for me. I wasn't alone any more. I'd found a new mate for life and it didn't matter for a single second that he lived inside a piece of black vinyl and that we could only meet up when I put him on the music centre in the middle of the living room.

When Paul Weller played guitar it was like fresh blood pumping through me and when he opened his mouth and sang it was like he'd been reading my diaries. How could this be only a coincidence? The lyrics were too personal and the music too perfect. I'd found The Jam, they were my band, my secret and they existed for me and me alone – I could not live without them, they were my lifeline out of being Lost in Leeds.

Night after night I sat at the dining room table with the volume on the stereo turned down, doing my homework whilst listening to The Jam. It was no good, though, The Jam were far from at their best when the volume's on two – it should have been on twelve. To appreciate them properly, I was going to need a stereo of my own, up in my room. With no birthday on the horizon and Christmas months away, I had to move fast if I was going to get Paul Weller up to my room and all on my own. I decided to embark on a period of being ultra-nice to Mum, Chris and Phil, but it wasn't too long before Mum twigged that I wanted something in return for being so polite and helping around the house so much more than normal: cleaning out the pond, raking up leaves, that sort of nonsense.

Mum had become sort of friendly in a know-to-say-hello-to kind of a way with a lady down the road who was an agent for Kay's catalogue and who'd signed Mum up as a member almost the day after we moved in. I think Mum did it just to get rid of her, but we could now order stuff from the catalogue – plus, it gave her someone to talk to.

I'd decided which one I wanted – a little Sony diskette which played seven- and twelve-inch records and – get this – you could stack up to ten singles on there at once. When each one finished, the next single dropped down on top and played automatically. It was excellent value at only thirty-four pounds and ninety-five pence. I showed it to Mum and she said that if I really, really wanted it and she got it for me then it'd have to come out of my pocket money. I said that that was fine and she ordered it the next day. Chris got a new Lego set and Phil got a cowboy outfit. I didn't know then, but thinking about it now perhaps it was her way of making me feel better about being in Leeds and being alone.

I spent the next few days gazing at it in the catalogue, flicking through the thin pages between the stereo and the lingerie section. I loved poring over the bras and knickers modelled by the lovely girls and I especially liked the ladies' shoes, all strappy and high with painted toenails peeking through. When the stereo came on the Saturday morning I couldn't have been more thrilled, because while I watched Dad set it up in my room, Mum came in and gave me my own copy of *This Is The Modern World*. I was bowled over and felt my bottom lip go – it felt like all of my birthdays had come at once. I had my own personal Paul all to myself.

My new stereo meant that I could lie on my bed and enjoy the delights of The Jam alone, in the privacy of my own room. I could lie there and read the lyrics from the sleeve and sing along without fear of embarrassment, I could stand in front of the mirror and mime along and pretend to play guitar with Dad's old wooden tennis racket, just like Paul did. After about a week of blasting out the whole house with my music, I was given another present, this time a pair of headphones. I got the message.

Recently, Dad had been spending more and more time away from home. He'd been in Germany for weeks on end at some sales conference or something, and when he finally came home he spent two days with us before zooming off to Wales for five days to see some clients. I understood that it was work, but that didn't stop me missing him all the same.

Mum had taken Chris and Phil swimming and I was in the house all on my own. I went into Mum and Dad's bedroom and laid down on their bed on Dad's side. I didn't switch on the light, I laid my head on his pillow in the darkness. I could smell his aftershave, I could smell his hair. I buried my face deep in the pillow and breathed in my Dad. 'I miss you.' I wished that I had a radio so that I could listen to him, listen to him at work with his customers like I did with the taxis.

I got up off the bed and opened the wardrobe door. Dad's suits hung on the rail. There was a black, shiny mohair one, three-buttoned with a narrow lapel and a single vent. Next was a slate grey wool number with a scarlet hanky in the breast pocket. Next to that was his midnight blue three-piece and then a load of shirts in crisp, white cotton, black silk and some pastels with button-down collars. His ties hung on a small brass rail inside the door and his shoes sat on a shelf above the suits.

I reached inside the wardrobe and gently stroked the

shoulder of the black mohair jacket. I'd always loved him in this, it made him shimmer when he walked, made him look like a film star. I slipped the jacket from the hanger, then the trousers and I laid them on the bed. Next out was the white shirt with the double cuff.

Off came my sweatshirt and down came my jeans. The shirt swallowed me up, the hem hung down below my knobbly knees and the tips of the collar pointed out behind my skinny little shoulders like I'd grown sharp, white wings. I hauled up his trousers and they were so big on me they could have gone round me twice, so I took the cord from his dressing gown and lashed it around my waist. I puffed out the shirt to cover the cord and on went the jacket. It weighed a ton and the sleeves were almost a foot too long for me. I wrapped them around me, right the way round my back and it felt like a pair of long, loving arms giving me a great big hug. I switched on the bedside lamp and chose a tie. There was a thin, jet black silk one amongst the gaudy paisley ones and it was this that I wanted.

I took it from the rail and then stood on the bed so that I could reach the shoes on the top shelf. I took out Dad's best pair, the handmade ones which Mum nearly fainted over when she found out how much they cost.I took the black ankle boots and slipped my feet inside my father's shoes. They were so big on me that I shuffled in them as I walked over to the mirror and tied my tie. I tied it in a nice, neat knot and I stood back and examined my reflection in the mirror. Dad stared right back at me.

I took a step back, startled. I spat into the palm of my hand and worked it into my hair. I spat again, and smoothed away the side parting I'd always had and spiked up my hair on the crown, a tuft now stuck up on top. I fixed it with a squirt of Mum's Silvikrin, loosened the knot on my tie and undid the top button on my shirt. I checked the mirror again and this time Dad was not there any more. Now it was Paul Weller who was staring back at me.

Slowly, I took off the shoes, the black jacket, the trousers, the shirt and the tie. I hung the trousers on the hanger and smoothed down the jacket. I felt something inside one of the pockets and dipped my hand in and pulled out a packet of Gold Leaf. The suit went back in the wardrobe but the smokes stayed with me. I turned out the light, closed the bedroom door and went quietly to my room.

* * *

Dad was back from Wales and it was time for my trim. I'd been dreading this for weeks – we all had the same haircuts, the same side partings in the same style just like Dad and Grampa Lines. The five of us all had the same hair. In fact, I'm surprised that Dad didn't insist on cutting Mum's the same way, too. We were up in the bathroom, and Phil had just had his done. Chris was playing in the bedroom next door which he shared with Phil. He was after me.

I sat on the stool and Dad slipped a towel around my shoulders. His cigarette burned in the ashtray on the windowsill, the smoke coiling up through the sunlight, slipping through the dusty blinds and I looked at the leather strap on the back of the bathroom door. I wanted to say something, wanted to ask him a question but when I opened my dry mouth all that came out was a squeak.

'What was that, Davey lad?'

'I want to ask you something.'

'What's that, then?'

'Dad, do you think that we could try a new style, please?'

There was silence between us in the bathroom. The dripping tap sounded like sonar and echoed like a gong.

'What kind of a new style? What's wrong with the way I cut your hair?' I felt his hands squeeze my shoulders through the towel.

'Nothing, Dad. Nothing wrong at all, just thought I'd try a new look.'

We caught each other's gaze in the mirror.

'A new look? What are you, lad, a girl?'

I could feel the sting of tears coming and I desperately tried to blink them away. 'No, Dad. I'm not a girl.'

He smiled a thin smile and told me to bow down my head and to keep very still. I did as I was told, and I knew then that he'd never cut my hair again, not in a million years.

2

To Be Someone

The third Jam album, *All Mod Cons*, came out in November 1978. I got it as an early Christmas present and had to ask for another one when Christmas came because I'd worn it out from playing it so much. This album was the turning point for The Jam, and rightly so. It was like a new Jam had been born, and with them the real start of the mod revival. The inner sleeve of the album dripped with mod imagery; scooters, targets, old Motown records, badges, and I found it all as fascinating as the music my three hero friends had made.

All Mod Cons was the turning point for me as well. It was when I decided to go the whole hog and get 'the look'. Being a fan of The Jam wasn't just about the music, it was the clothes, the hair, the shoes, the detail – above all, it was about the detail.

Paul had inspired me to want to look sharp at all times, and I wasn't about to go and mess it up by not looking right. At school, there were parkas everywhere. Overnight, the modernist revival had spread north from London and before I knew it, it felt as if half the school were wearing Fred Perry shirts, narrow, straight-legged jeans, parkas and white socks. Of course, that wasn't the case, it just felt as if they were. I felt invaded, robbed of The Jam now that everyone else had got into them, so now was the time to join the army of mods at school and help reclaim the band as my own. I began with the Kay's catalogue.

The first items we ordered constituted my Christmas presents, and I went for two red Fred Perrys, both with blue motif and matching piping on the collar and sleeves as well as a pair of straight-leg Levi's jeans. I'd only got little legs, and Mum told me when we placed the order that she'd have to take them up for me, but that didn't matter because she was good with a sewing machine, and she said it wouldn't take long. I was doing all that I could to get Paul's look right. At the time, I couldn't really care less about the mod movement – for me, it was about The Jam and about me connecting with Paul. It was only after I went on to discover how much mod meant to Paul through reading interviews with him that it started to rub off onto me, get under my skin and deep, deep into my soul.

The success which Paul, Bruce and Rick were having had sparked a frenzy of mod revivalist bandwagon bands, such as The Chords, Secret Affair, Purple Hearts, Squire and The Merton Parkas, although some of these were true mod groups who'd been around as long as The Jam. Squire are still going strong to this day, and I liked their song 'Walking Down The King's Road' as well as Secret Affair's 'My World' and 'Time For Action', but none of them ever came close to The Jam for me. There was something special, something which acted as a beacon for me with The Jam, they were my everything and their music helped guide and shape me in those early lost days in Leeds. If I'm honest, it still guides me today. Whenever I'm in doubt or the dark clouds gather I'll listen to Weller and, soon enough, all will be well again.

Button badges were essential in creating 'the look' and Wide-a-Wake records was *the* place to get them in Garforth. I remember my first visit. Wide-a-Wake was situated on Main Street, sandwiched between Motor World, with its tiny steering wheels lined up in the window like little leather-covered shirt buttons, and Thurston's Bakers which had a poster up in its window that read 'Three Sausage Rolls for 20p'. I opened the door and stepped inside; the pressure mat triggered Gary Glitter singing 'Hello, hello, it's good to be back, good to be back.' I couldn't believe how small the shop was, almost like a booth, with the back wall entirely covered by an enormous poster of Kate Bush wearing a lilac leotard and staring down at me from behind the counter. She looked lovely, but she also looked like she'd escaped from some sort of secure mental health unit.

After a minute, a man's voice came from behind a curtain drawn behind the counter: 'I'll be out in a minute. But if you're here for The Three Degrees you're out of luck – they're not coming in till Monday.' I walked over to the record racks and there, under 'J', was *All Mod Cons* and behind it, *In The City* and *This Is The Modern World*. I had to check to make sure that they were there. It's a comfort thing, and I still do it to this day when I'm in a record store. Paul stared out at me from the sleeve, all moody with a brutal crew cut, shirt buttoned up, as hard and cool and crisp and clean as they come. He looked hard, rock hard, like the sort of friend I could have done with having, living there in Garforth. It was grim up north, grim and hard but not as hard as Paul – he'd look after me. I smiled at him and slipped him back into the rickety rack.

I spent ages trying to decide which button badges to buy. They cost twenty-five pence each and I'd enough money for two. God, there were so many to choose from and it was a good three-quarters of an hour before I finally made up my mind and plumped for a mod target with an arrow sticking out of the top and one with 'The Jam' spray-painted in black onto a white background. I pinned them onto the sleeve of my parka and set off home as proud as punch.

It wasn't a fishtail parka. In fact it wasn't even green. It was a blue snorkel parka from the catalogue and felt like lagging from an industrial boiler unit. If I zipped the thing up I could actually feel myself melting. I made myself a promise to get my wardrobe in order – the mod movement was well under way at school and if I was going to be a proper Jam fan then I needed to look the part – and I'm sorry, but a blue snorkel parka with a couple of button badges just wasn't going to do it.

It was half five in the afternoon and Mum was having a Tia Maria whilst trying to muster up enough energy to tackle the pile of ironing on the kitchen table. An almighty heap, shirts and trousers all tangled together – there could have been someone buried in there.

'Mum?'

'Yes, dear?'

'I need to get some new white socks.'

'White socks?'

'That's right. I need three pairs of white *towelling* socks.'

She put down her drink and raised an eyebrow. 'You need white towelling socks? Sports socks?'

'That's it exactly. Sports socks. But they must be towelling and they must be white.'

'But you don't do sport. You avoid it like the plague.'

'That's not the point, Mum. And I also need to get my hands on a boating blazer. It's a matter of some urgency.'

'A *boating* blazer? Have you been reading *Brideshead*

Revisited again? And anyway, we just got you the snorkel parka at Christmas.'

'And bowling shoes. I must have some bowling shoes, it's absolutely essential I get my feet into a pair of bowling shoes. Now, where's the Kay's catalogue?'

In all honesty I don't know if falling in love with shoes was down to my becoming a mod or down to my father and his love of what he put on his feet. Whatever the cause, shoes were becoming a big part of my relationship with Paul Weller. After bowling shoes came Clark's desert boots. These were the real starting point.

Clark's desert boots were classics; easy to wear, easy on the eye, steeped in history, went well with whatever trousers you were wearing, ultra-comfy, came in a variety of super-cool colours and, most importantly of all – available from the Kay's catalogue. Plus, Paul seemed to wear them all the time. I begged and begged and begged and finally got a pair of beige ones after promising faithfully to look after them and never ever wear them in the rain. I slopped Heinz tomato ketchup on the left toe within half an hour of putting them on. It absolutely would not shift, not even when Dad applied his specialist dry-cleaning knowledge, which basically consisted of him emptying a bottle of turps on the stain and then drying it with a hairdryer. Rubbish. It still looked as if I'd shot myself in the foot.

That night, after tea, I was up in my bedroom listening to *All Mod Cons* again. It's as brilliant now as it was when I first heard it. It's got everything. It's just the most complete set of songs that I've ever heard and think that I ever will. There's so much of me in it, sometimes I have to take it off because it's almost too much for me to take. The single 'Down In The Tube Station At Midnight' was banned from Radio One by that idiot disc jockey Tony Blackburn because he thought it glorified violence. It doesn't, it renounces violence. It tells the story of a young, married man going home on the Tube and getting set upon by a group of louts who kick seven shades out of him after robbing him and taking his keys, and then his poor wife thinks it's her husband letting himself in. The thugs smell of pubs, and Wormwood Scrubs and too many right-wing meetings. It's terrifying, so powerful, so graphic. There are sound effects of the train on the tracks, pulling in and out of the station. It's like listening to a horror movie, and it gets more and more harrowing every time I hear it.

Then, in contrast, there's 'English Rose'. This is just Paul on an acoustic guitar instead of a caustic guitar. This is the most perfect love song that I could ever possibly imagine. It's fragile and delicate and simple and complex all at the same time. This song actually sounds like a bruise. The first time I heard this track I could barely hold back the tears, not least because I couldn't help wonder whether I'd ever feel like that about another human being. Paul wrote this whilst touring the States in the spring of 1978, locked away in hotel rooms because he was too young to go out and get trashed in the bars with the older guys who were part of the tour. They kept him supplied with beer while he stayed locked away, and from behind those anonymous hotel room doors came this sweet, soulful ballad.

Weller never sang this song live whilst in The Jam. He even recorded it in an empty studio when he put down the vocal – I can understand that; baring your soul, especially when you've got such a hard and flinty image, must have been almost impossible for him. You can tell it's written by a lonely soul, touring the world, marvelling at new sights which take your breath away and yet missing like mad the one you love and the place you come from. There's a foghorn on there, which heralds the arrival of the writer back to where he lives, stepping off the boat and returning to the place he calls home. Lovely. I'd listen to it and lie back on my bed, close my eyes and imagine being back in Bridgford with the tree-lined boulevards and gentle, friendly faces instead of the cold, lonely lights of Leeds.

I turned down the music and sneaked across the landing into my parents' room. I could hear everyone downstairs and I made for the chest of drawers. I was looking for a new item of clothing to add to my new look, my Jam Outfit. Suddenly Mum's voice came at me, out of the dark of the unlit landing. She was standing in the doorway with a Silk Cut on the go.

'What are you doing rooting around in your father's clothes for?'

'I'm looking for a black tie.'

Mum took a drag and asked, 'Who died?'

'Nobody's died. It's a fashion statement. Where does Dad keep his very narrow black ties?'

'Are you playing at being James Bond again? Because if you are, your old water pistol's somewhere under the sink . . .'

I went in the bathroom and stared at my reflection

in the mirror. I absolutely hated my stupid hair. The side parting felt like it'd been branded into the side of my thin head and it really was time to go. To hell with the consequences – it was coming off. I knew that Dad'd make me change it back in an instant, just like the time when I wanted a change. 'What are you – a girl?' I opened the cabinet and took out his scissors. It all came very naturally to me, like I was on autopilot. It was clear that hairdressing was in the blood, and very soon I was making a highly professional job of delivering a mighty fine haircut indeed. I wanted a crew cut like the one Paul had, and by the time I was finished, mine would be identical.

My hair covered the bathroom carpet and what was left on my head was about half an inch long. The back was a problem, basically because I couldn't see what I was doing, so I took out the cut-throat razor and ran it under the hot tap.

The razor had a yellowed bone handle and was as light as a feather in the palm of my hand. It slid effortlessly down my hair and great clumps fell to the floor. With just four or five strokes the back was done and even though I knew it'd be shorter round there than up on top, I was confident of a good result. I ran the sink full of warm water and dunked my head right the way in to rinse off the snippets. I dried my hair on the hand towel and it all stuck up on top like the loo brush. It wasn't bad at all to say that I'd done it myself, and I wasn't only pleased, I felt strangely empowered. I took the wooden hand mirror from the shelf and held it up to inspect my handiwork round the back of my head.

These weren't the results I was looking for. I looked like a trainee Cistercian monk. There was nothing there at all but smooth skin. The back of my head looked like a huge bollock. Or Darth Vader without his helmet on. This was not the ideal look with which to go downstairs and prove to my father that I was now old enough for him not to cut my hair any more. But I had to be a man about it and face the situation head on. There was no way I could hide what I had done and because my descent downstairs would be only marginally less painful than entering Hell, with uncontrollable howls of laughter from Chris and Phil, screams of horror from Mum and the terrible, eardrum-shattering silence from Dad, I put it off till morning and went straight to bed. I hid under the covers and listened to them enjoying something on the television, their peals of laughter snaking up the stairs and keeping me from sleep.

Next day the true horror of the haircut revealed itself to the outside world. I came down for breakfast, sat at the table and poured Rice Krispies into a bowl. Chris and Phil were eating their cereal whilst Dad polished his shoes. Mum mashed tea in the pot and Chris asked, 'Why are you wearing my balaclava?'

Through a maw full of breakfast came my rehearsed reply. 'I'm coming down with something. I think I've got a head cold.'

Dad stopped his polishing and removed the balaclava. As he did so cornflakes came out of Chris's nose and Phil sprayed orange juice everywhere. Phil pointed at me, giggling like a loon, and told me that I looked like Beaker, the scientist's assistant in *The Muppets*. This hurt, as I didn't want to look like Beaker – I wanted to look like Paul Weller from The Jam. Mum said, 'You silly, silly boy.' And I looked up at Dad who simply stared down at me, then shook his head, looked away, turned on his heel and walked out of the door. He didn't say a word and he didn't slam the door. The silence was enough, and it echoed through the house.

When he went, Chris said, 'Don't worry, it's not

such a bad hairstyle.' Phil said, 'You're right, it's not too bad.' Chris said, 'Actually, you know, it's not brilliant,' and Phil came back with, 'Come to think of it, it is pretty dreadful.' They were enjoying playing at being the two grumpy old Muppets up in the balcony and I left for school to the sound of them singing the theme tune.

If it was going to be that bad at home, then turning up at Garforth Comprehensive was going to be a whole lot worse. My only option was the chemist's shop at the end of Fairburn Drive where I bought a roll of bandage with some of my dinner money.

I nipped round the back of the shops and wrapped the bandage around my head, securing it in place with my Jam button badge. It was the only plausible way of avoiding having the living piss ripped out of me for looking so ridiculous. For the next six weeks I slipped into my disguise when I left the house and out of it as I walked up the drive at the end of the day. Whenever anyone asked what I'd done, I just said that I'd fallen off my bike.

As my hair grew back, Dad began talking to me again. The more it grew, the more he spoke to me. I used to have imaginary conversations with Paul where he'd sit on the end of my bed and we'd chat about all sorts of stupid things, like what kind of shampoo he used and where he bought his shoes from and nonsense like that. I liked these chats in my head and they kept me sane when Dad wasn't talking to me and I was feeling lonely and left out at school.

Before Leeds I really liked school life. I was pretty popular, got good grades and was finding myself. Once we'd moved, however, I went inside myself, retreated, I suppose. I knew that I had to try and make some proper friends, not just pupils to chat to, or I'd go mad. I always ended up making a pig's ear of it, though. Walking home after school down the disused railway track seemed like a good place to start. I decided to make conversation with someone, anyone, as a test for myself to prove I could do it. The problem was, that the one time I'd promised myself I'd make an effort, I suddenly developed hay fever.

It was mid-May 1979, everything out in bud and the tree and grass pollen made my eyes itch to the point where I wanted to tear them out of their bright red, sore sockets and fling them into the white flowers of the hawthorn bushes that made them swell up and sting so. The more I scratched my eyes, the worse they became. When I got home, Mum almost fainted when she saw me. 'Oh, my poor boy! Come here at once!' She put her arms around me and started to sob; when she pulled away from my face she examined me closely. 'Who did this to you? You tell me right now which big oaf did this to you and believe you me, his sorry little life won't be worth living. Now, how did you get in such a fight? You were sticking up for yourself, weren't you?' Mum could barely hold back the tears as she stared at my puffy, purple, swollen face.

'It's the grass, Mum, the grass did it to me.'

She suddenly looked disappointed. 'Oh. I thought you might have been in a fight or something . . .' I felt that if I'd been in a fight, at least she'd be happy that I'd been mixing with other kids. She went to the fridge, opened the door, took out a cucumber and cut me two slices. 'Here, put these on your eyes. And you can stick the rest in a cheese sarnie if you like . . .' What a wasted trip down the railway track that was; it's a good job I didn't meet anyone looking like that.

At school the next day, it was double woodwork first thing. My eyes looked like two black balloons. I was trying to make a toast rack. It wasn't easy when I could hardly see. I'd been trying to make this toast rack for what seemed like ages and it looked nothing like a toast rack, or it wouldn't if I could actually see it. What it looked like was two pieces of plywood glued together with a length of dowelling stuck between them at the base.

Mr Armitage, the woodwork teacher, stood next to me and cast a professional eye over my clearly unprofessional job. As it stood, one piece of lightly done Sunblest would bring the thing crashing to its knees. He didn't look impressed.

'Remind me never to have breakfast at your house, Lines.'

I was astonished that he even knew my name.

'Sorry, sir?'

'Been busy scrapping, have we? A right couple of shiners you've got there. You need to learn to keep your guard up.'

I could have told him that flowers and not fists were responsible, but instead I just agreed with him and got back to making a dog's dinner of the rack. It was so much easier to appear a puncher than a pansy.

After break, it was double music. We were learning to play the recorder. Mr Hinkley, Head of Music, was in charge of the class. He wore rose-tinted spectacles and tight, bum-hugging Farah slacks. I needed to get my hair right before class, so went to the loo at the last minute to wet it and spike it up at the back, just like Paul's. The procedure was a private one, and required the solitude afforded by an empty boys' bog, free from the ridicule of spectators and piss-takers. I took the opportunity to shine the heels of my burgundy loafers and readjust my white socks nice and straight. My tie was reversed, the thick bit at the back and stuffed inside my (buttoned-down) white shirt, the thin, narrow end left out on display. I looked good, but was almost ten minutes late for the start of the lesson.

When I finally got to room thirty-seven, D-block, I opened the music-room door and there, sitting right on the front row, were Adam Ant, Sting and Gary Numan – all busy learning to play a plastic recorder. I took a moment to take the picture in; it was an eclectic ensemble, after all. I made my apologies and took a seat. Gary Numan wasn't actually Gary Numan, he was, in fact, Gary Newman – and his dad delivered our milk at home. Sting's real name was Stuart Gowlet whose mum was away at a special hospital somewhere ever since his dad went to prison for doing something unspeakable but nobody knew exactly what. And Adam Ant? Adam Ant was really Julie Westerman.

So many people all wanting to be someone else. Ridiculous. What on earth's wrong with them? Had they no personality? I took a double take at Julie Westerman. She might have had the hair, she might have had the same sort of androgynous features as Adam Ant, but today something was off. Thinking back on it now, I realise that Julie had taken Adam Ant's look to its logical conclusion and had predicted his future image – the Dandy Highwayman one – but at the time, she just looked like a pretty, punkish Dick Turpin. She sat there with two red stripes across each cheek, loads of little coloured braids in her hair and her cloak draped over the chair beside her. She playfully twiddled the highwayman mask around her little finger and her clarinet box lay closed, on the floor next to her pixie-booted feet. I paused before sitting down to wonder if it may well not contain her clarinet, but a pair of early nineteenth-century flintlocks.

I sat down. 'Hi, Jules.'

'Alright, Linesy.'

Linesy? That wasn't bad – my black eye was beginning to open some doors for me.

'And where's Black Bess this morning, then?'

'Very funny.'

'No, seriously, I was just wondering, because if you've tied her up round the back of the bike shed, she'll probably be needing some fresh water by now. It's a real sun trap in there at this time of day.'

'Fuck off.'

I turned my attention to Gary Numan who was busy staring at his recorder as if trying to communicate with the thing through the power of thought alone. He once told me that he truly believed himself to be not entirely one hundred per cent human. Watching him then, I could believe it.

Mr Hinkley passed a white plastic cup around the class. It was full of pink liquid which smelled of bleach and we all dunked the mouthpieces of our recorders in, then wiped them on a tissue. When we'd all finished, he addressed us from behind his rosy red glasses. He was leaning against a baby grand piano, one hand resting on the top of it holding the plastic cup, the other on his hip, which stuck out at quite an angle. His grey Farah slacks seemed particularly tight that day and he'd teamed them up with a light, pink shirt and a cream silk scarf tied around his long, thin neck. He said,

'Right, boys and girls – today, I want us to concentrate on our fingering techniques.'

After music was lunch, and I took my hot dog, chips, milkshake and vanilla ice cream and got a seat at a table which posed no threat. That is, I didn't know anyone else at it. I sat down and took a bite out of my cold, rubbery sausage wrapped in its claggy, wet bread roll and looked up to meet the faces of two greasy, fat biker types. They did not look happy. In fact, they looked about as happy with me as I was with my lunch. I looked away and took another bite, squirting ketchup on my chips just for something to do. There were other tables, so why did I go and pick this one? I chewed on the chips, made the mistake of looking up and came face to face with the heaviest of the heavies. He had a chip stuffed up each nostril, and they hung down over each side of his mouth and he was pulling some sort of daft Dracula face at me. He held my gaze and opened his wet mouth. The words dripped out like pus from one of his many pores. 'You're a poncey mod.' I certainly was – and that meant looking sharp at all times and not taking any shit from anyone. Especially this tramp.

'Yep. And you're a scruffy, fat greaser . . . and to make things worse, you have food hanging out of your nose. You really should deal with it – that's not a cool look, even for someone like you. Actually, I'm glad we're here together, because I want to ask you a question.'

'What?'

'Have you ever heard of shampoo?' The ape looked at his mate and then back at me, blinking slowly. His slack jaw, the wet goo dribbling out of the corner of his acned mouth, the filthy denim jacket with 'Blackmore Is God' embroidered on the back, the lank, unbrushed hair, the sickly stench of patchouli – he just looked like everything I'd rather die than be. There was a moment, and it hung in the fug of the busy dining hall like a finger on a trigger. Finally, he grunted again, 'What?'

'Shampoo. You put it on your head and you wash your hair with it. Try it – you never know, it might even make you look like a human being.'

He stared at his mate and then back at me and I stood up before he did, turned on my heel and walked slowly away. It was a cool move, and was made even more so because hanging around any longer would almost certainly have resulted in me being stretchered out of there and taken by air ambulance to Seacroft District Hospital.

Maybe it was the gall, maybe it was the idiocy of mouthing off in front of them, maybe it was me growing into my role as a mod, I don't know – what I do remember is that at some point around this time I regained my confidence. I wore my Jam button badges like an old soldier would wear the George Cross – with pride and with style – and my loafers seemed to carry me so much taller from that day on. There were a lot of rude boys at Garforth Comp, a lot of punks and some serious skins, as well as a lot in fifth and sixth forms who were still big into prog rock. Rockabillie was around as well, with Matchbox trying to get a fifties revival going, probably off the back of *Grease*. I'm not even sure that those of us who were mods even knew the real, subtle differences right at the start. It was, and still is, a secret little code. If you got it wrong, there'd always be the chance for embarrassment. But when you got it right, it just felt so good inside, so . . . natural.

I didn't know what to put it down to; the music, modernism, The Jam, me growing into me being me, whatever – but within a few months I had two new things. A girlfriend and a new best mate. One that didn't live inside a piece of plastic.

3

The Eton Rifles

Whenever I hear this track now, whatever I'm doing, it always takes me there, carries me back to the first time that I heard it. It came crashing through my bedroom speakers like the three of them had just kicked the front door in, and made me feel like I could run right through a plate glass window at a hundred miles an hour. It felt like a call to arms, and even though I didn't get the humour in it till maybe the fourth or fifth play, it awoke an interest in socialism, in kitchen-sink politics and class warfare – stuff that at school I wouldn't have come close to till the sixth form, a good five years off.

'The Eton Rifles' was released in October 1979. I was twelve – just sixteen weeks away from my thirteenth birthday. Paul wrote it on holiday at his mum and dad's caravan down in Selsey Bill. It's like two-dozen cannons going off and thunders along with Paul screeching and feeding back the Rickenbacker, Rick spraying out drum fills and Bruce punctuating it with an intricate, thumping bass. Some songs make you want to get up and dance but this isn't one of them. This is a song that makes you want to start a fire. Or a revolution. I've just played it whilst writing this and it's left me breathless. Twenty-five years later and still it makes me want to turn the world upside down. I'll have a go when I've finished my tax return.

Paul said in an interview with the *Eton College Chronicle* of Friday, 16 November, 1979 that he hoped he hadn't upset anyone there, not intentionally. The interviewer said that no, on the contrary, students were buying it like mad and Paul said that that was great, and that maybe they'd get to number one with it. They didn't, they got to number three, which was a shame, because for my money it was the best number one hit single which The Jam never had. The flip side, however, was a different matter entirely.

'See-Saw' is light and without direction and comes nowhere near close to the standard of other Jam B-sides. Maybe they wanted to keep new material fresh for the upcoming *Setting Sons* album, maybe the record company didn't feel they needed a quality track as such to backup something as strong as 'The Eton Rifles'. I'm not so sure about this theory, because Polydor clearly weren't behind the record from the start. Unimaginable, I know. The truth of the matter is Polydor thought the single far too political to get any airplay on the BBC and essentially walked away from it. Typical Weller – he fired the record company's promotional people and brought in another promoter, Clive Banks. Banks worked his magic, the record got played and the rest is history. Truth be told, whatever appeared on the B-side would never live up to the A-side. Even 'Eleanor Rigby' would have paled next to 'The Eton Rifles'. If *All Mod Cons* was the defining album for them, this, then, was their defining single.

It was an evil year, 1979. Margaret Thatcher became the first woman Prime Minister. I didn't like her for two reasons: her voice and her hair. I could laugh, though. I laughed at *Not The Nine O'Clock News* and howled at one particular sketch. In it, Griff Rhys-Jones did a piece straight to camera, his face full-frame. He talked like a right old yob, with a sneering, curled top lip and a surly look that said, 'Come and have a go if you think you're hard enough.' He went on about going down to Brighton at the weekend and looking forward to a proper scrap, and the camera pulled back a little and we saw his dark jacket, dark tie and short haircut and you thought, he's a mod. Then he went on a bit more, about the pitched battles on the pebble beach and how him and his mates love a right ruck, and the camera finally pulled back to reveal that he's a copper. I laughed out loud at home, but nobody else did.

A few weeks after my thirteenth birthday. Early afternoon on a bright, spring Saturday. I was getting ready to take Fiona McLelland out on a date and I could hardly believe my luck. Not too many of the other boys in my class had girlfriends, and it took me ages to muster up the courage to ask Fiona out. She sat next to me in maths and we playfully flirted for a while before I finally asked her out. She was tall and slender, with multicoloured hair and enormous feet which she crammed into flat winkle-pickers and she had a nice, big, warm, wobbly smile. We'd been going out with each other for two weeks and in that time we'd spoken four times on the phone and been to Youth Club together twice. Mum and Dad were a bit bemused by me having a real-life girlfriend, but it wasn't anything to worry about, they were happy that I was finally settling in. They were also very eager to meet Fiona, although I got the feeling that they thought I'd actually invented her.

Youth Club (or 'Youthy') was on three nights a week in the sixth-form block – 'The Link'. There was a disco in one room, table tennis in another, five-a-side outside and lots of snogging inside. Fiona and I hadn't snogged yet, but we had held hands and pecked each other on the cheek quite a bit, and I was hoping that on that afternoon we'd get over that hurdle.

We met at the school gates and went for a romantic walk up Main Street. Fiona wore jeans, winkle-pickers and a big, baggy cream jumper. I wore my Levi's jeans, white moccasins and a red Fred Perry tennis shirt with blue trim and a blue logo, and I spent nearly two hours getting my hair right before I left the house. We held hands and talked about school and music and clothes and we wandered into Wide-a-Wake records and had a look around. I bought Fiona a Jam button badge but she said that that was far too kind and generous of me and that, no, really, I should keep it for myself – she couldn't possibly accept it.

We went to the baker's and I treated us both to a chocolate eclair and a can of Coke to share. We ate the eclairs walking down the street. I liked Main Street on Saturday afternoons. Some of the shops shut for the day at lunchtime and this left the place half deserted. A paper bag blew towards us, the wind caught it and carried it up, high above our heads. Dust in the gutter swirled, and Fiona had cream from her eclair on the faint, golden moustache above her oh-so-kissable top lip. She was freckly, and that day the sun had caught her face and covered it with them. Mum had a freckly face, but not that freckly. Fiona looked even nicer than normal that Saturday. I felt nice, too, and fought the urge to lick the cream off her face like a cat.

There was something that I had to do, and I didn't want to raise the subject for fear of upsetting Fiona and I knew that if I did, and I really did have to, then I'd go and spoil everything, and that was not a day that I wanted to ruin. But it couldn't be avoided any longer . . .

A couple of days previously, Mum had been cleaning my room when she came down and asked me where the Madness album was that Granny and Grampa Sewter had bought me for my birthday.

'I've given it to Fiona.'

'You've given it away?'

'That's right. To my girlfriend.'

Mum looked far from pleased. 'Oh. Why?'

'Well, it wasn't really my kind of thing. There were only a couple of songs on there that I really liked, and I didn't even ask for it in the first place . . .'

Mum lit a cigarette and poured some lemon barley water into a glass tumbler. She took a drag and smoke came hurtling out of both nostrils like she'd turned into some sort of dragon. 'Good God, David – that was a birthday present from your Granny. She went and bought that herself because she thought it was the sort of thing that you were into. And you go and give it away? Just like that? You ungrateful boy. I'm very cross with you – very, very cross.'

I was stunned. Mum very rarely spoke to any of us like that. The thought that I'd upset her upset me more than what I'd done and I wanted to cry like a little baby. My bottom lip went and she said, 'It's no good turning on the water works, I'm not going to forgive you for giving that record away. Your Granny went to a lot of time and trouble and effort in getting it for you, going into Nottingham on the bus and buying it. They came up especially, you know, to bring it for your birthday because they worried that if they'd posted it, it'd get broken. You ungrateful, selfish boy . . .'

Mum hadn't said very much to me at all since then. I wanted to make things better between us, so I came up with this great idea to try and calm the troubled waters. It was brilliant. What I was *not* going to do, was to ask Fiona for the Madness album back. That would be childish and rude and unfair on her. I'd also end up looking like a prize idiot. No, what I *had* decided to do, was to ask her for the money for it . . .

We'd walked to the top of Main Street and were now halfway back down the other side, heading towards school. The paper bag was following us. Sometimes it caught us up and got ahead of us, and then it'd float back down to the ground and pretend to look in a shop window or it would get caught up against a lamp post as if it thought we hadn't noticed it.

'Don't look now, but it's stopped for some chips.'

Fiona laughed and squeezed my hand. 'Do you fancy going up onto the cricket pitch?'

'Can do. Do you fancy opening the batting, or shall I?'

Fiona held my gaze and said, 'You can open if you want to.'

God, this sounded promising.

Ten minutes later we were sitting on the cricket pitch, making a daisy chain. The sun grew brighter, but an even stronger breeze blew so I shuffled round in front of Fi so that my back acted as a windbreak for her. She reached out and took my face in her hands. She gently pulled me towards her and we kissed, softly, for maybe ten seconds or so. Her tongue was hot and stiff and it didn't so much slip as *drill* into my mouth, and then she closed her lips around my tongue and sucked so hard that I was petrified she'd tear the thing out by the root. I think it was the tears of pain streaming down my face which finally gave the game away and Fiona quickly released me from her suction grasp. 'Sorry, David. Did I hurt you? Are those real tears?'

'No, that was just lovely, thanks. You're a great kisser. It's just my hay fever playing up. Um, shall we go, then?'

Fiona sounded surprised at this. 'Go? We've only just got here. Come here, you . . .'

She slipped her arm around my neck and this time the kiss was much softer. The only problem was, it'd been going on for about four and a half minutes and we sort of ended up breathing through one another's mouths. I didn't even know that this was physically possible, and although it was far from unpleasant, it did take a bit of getting used to. Fiona was absolutely scarlet in the face by then, and when she did finally manage to disentangle me from her wet mouth, she fell back onto the grass, grabbing my hand and taking me with her.

I lay on top of her, and she kind of rubbed herself against my leg and breathed very fast. She took off her jumper. There was a thin white blouse underneath and she undid the top three buttons. Her chest was freckly, too. I could see her bra strap through it, white and lacy. I wanted to see her bra. I wanted to get into it and feel what was inside. Was it too early for us? 'Is there something you want to ask me, Davey Boy?' She undid the top button of her jeans and smiled the sweetest, dirtiest of smiles. I could see the top of her knickers. They were purple, and I wanted to know everything about what went on inside them. I could hardly believe that this was actually happening to me.

I lay next to her. There were butterflies on top of the daisies and deep inside my stomach. This was to be the moment. 'Yeah,' I panted, 'can I have four quid for that Madness album?'

My clumsiness on the cricket pitch didn't go unnoticed. On the way into school the following Monday morning, Michelle Parker, Fiona's best friend, rushed up and pushed an envelope into my hand and then ran away. I opened the envelope and read the letter: Fiona had finished with me. Folded inside was a five pound note, and along the bottom of it, directly underneath the Duke of Wellington, Fiona had written, in blue biro, 'To a Crap Kisser.'

At long last, I'd made a new, male friend. His name was Richard Bowerman and he'd got a haircut just like Bruce Foxton's. He looked like he was wearing a busby on top of his head. Rik, as I renamed him, was almost as big a fan of The Jam as I was. He was in my class, but had only recently stopped wearing massive, rectangular spectacles. I couldn't have possibly spoken to him whilst he had those things perched on the end of his hooter. He looked like Grampa's greenhouse. And he had a side parting. Then, one Monday morning he came into class with his new fluffy head and no geeky glasses and he'd painted the most fabulous picture of The Jam onto his canvas haversack. Using a mixture of Humbrol model paints and heavy marker pens, Rik had recreated the front cover of the second single by The Jam, 'The Modern World'. I was both impressed and wildly jealous, although when you got in close for a really good look, he'd managed to make Bruce Foxton look more like Bruce Forsyth. It was actually rather disturbing.

Whilst Margaret Thatcher settled into her new role as Prime Maniac, the charts were full of The Village People, 'Bright Eyes' by Simon and Garfunkel was everywhere and Gloria Gaynor's 'I Will Survive' seemed to say goodbye to disco whilst punk and new wave danced, or rather pogoed, on its grave. But we didn't care, me and Rik. We were locked away in our little world, the world of The Jam and no one else was allowed to go there. We spent ages locked away in his bedroom making endless compilation tapes of our favourite songs by the best band in the world. We made different sorts of tapes for different styles of songs. There were punky, loud crashing tapes and then there were ballady, love song compilations. We made cassettes with songs on in order of how we rated them and we spent hours cutting out pictures of Paul, Bruce and Rick and designing our own special cover inserts for the tape boxes. We even made spine inserts with our own compilation titles on. We talked forever about The Jam, whole days were lost to them.

'What do you think Paul was like at school?'

'Um, I don't think that he rated it, to be honest.'

'Me neither. Do you think that he always knew he was going to be in a band?'

'Probably. You couldn't be that talented and not, you know, know.'

'No, I know. Which is your fave song on *Setting Sons*?'

'Tricky one, that. Probably . . . probably "Thick As Thieves".'

'Yeah, me too, Rik. Which is your fave bit in it?'

'Oh, God. Um, I think maybe the quieter, slower bit in the middle where Paul sings about stealing lovely young girls from ivory towers, stealing autumn rain and summer showers.'

'Yeah, it's brilliant that bit, isn't it?'

'Yeah, brilliant.'

'And I like "Private Hell" too. I love it when that woman has that nervous breakdown. It's great . . .'

'Yeah, I love that song. Hey – I've just had a brilliant idea.'

'What?'

'Let's go and polish our shoes . . .'

I spent forever round at Rik's. It was nice being in a different house, especially one which seemed so enormous compared to ours. I'm sure that Mum and Dad, Dad especially, were fed up with me wanting to spend time at someone else's house instead of at home. 'What's so special round there, anyway? What have they got that we haven't?' The answer was space to ourselves. Rik had an elder sister, Susan, but she'd moved out and got married years ago and his mum and dad were often out and even if they weren't, we hardly ever saw them because the place was so gigantic. It was like ASDA in there.

4

Going Underground

I turned the page of the *NME* and came to a piece all about the next single from The Jam. It was called 'Going Underground' and I ate it up. This was recorded in January 1980 down at the Townhouse Studios, deep in Shepherd's Bush, and was produced, again, by Vic Coppersmith-Heaven. It was to be released as the next single on 7 March – and I was going to be first in the queue for it. 'Going Underground',when it finally did see the light of day, was a double A-side. But more of that in a minute.

The Jam were touring the States when it crashed in at number one – and I helped put it there. With my own money. Just. There were advance orders for 200,000 copies – this was, literally, unheard of. When the news came through they aborted the tour and immediately got on a plane to get back to Blighty to record a performance for *Top Of The Pops*.

There were a whole five more days to wait till it was released and the article also reported that Paul had set up a company – Riot Stories – which was going to publish Youth Poetry. It included details of where to send your submissions and before I'd even finished reading the piece I was out of our front door and en route, on foot, to the newsagents to buy new pens and a pad.

I was very proud of my first poem for Paul. It took me all of ten minutes to compose and three further days to write it up in my best handwriting. I 'borrowed' my father's fountain pen from the bureau and wrote it out on Basildon Bond's best, torn from my mother's pad which she kept in the second drawer down in the Welsh dresser in the dining room.

You Know the Truth.

You think that you know us,
You think you can lead us,
But all that you do is,
Bleed and mislead us.

You were only a shopkeeper's daughter,
But I know you'll lead us to the slaughter,
So I really think I ought'a
Point out you're in really deep water.

You may well live in Number Ten,
With your gin-guzzling husband, Den,
But believe me one day we'll get you out,
And you may well scream and kick and shout,
But don't be left without a doubt,
You're just a big-haired stupid Tory trout.

Paul would be so impressed. I ran down the road and stuck it in the postbox. With a bit of luck, he'd get it in the morning . . .

The week before 'Going Underground' was released, there was an *incident*. I can remember it like it was only this morning. It was Friday night at Youthy, and there was a buzz in the air. Somehow Nick Wright had got hold of an advance copy of the single. He knew someone who worked for HMV in the centre of Leeds and they got their stocks delivered that morning.

I'd never spoken to Nick, but he was probably the most famous mod face in Garforth. He left school the previous summer to work as a window dresser and that night he was there, wearing a dark blue Crombie overcoat with a red silk hanky in the breast pocket. Nick Wright oozed style and I wanted to go and say hello and ask him what the new single sounded like but the word floating around Youthy was that Nick was going to play it at nine o'clock, so I decided to wait to hear it until then. It was twenty to eight.

Rik and I had arranged to meet next to the pool table at quarter to. I bought a can of Coke and by the time I got back to the meeting point, Rik was already there. He was wearing his black and yellow Fred Perry shirt and had obviously just blow-dried his hair, because it was extra fluffy. There was also something vaguely different about him, but at the time I just could not quite put my finger on it. 'Rik, man. You'll never guess what's happening here tonight.'

'Stands back in amazement. Go on, surprise me.' He took the can from my hand and had a big gulp of my Coke.

'Nick Wright's only somehow gone and got hold of an advance copy of "Going Underground" and he's playing it – right here – in just over one hour's time.'

Rik, mid-gulp, spun around and did a pretty dramatic, 360 degree comedy spray of the contents of his mouth, except that this was not a comedy moment, it was a Very Big Moment Indeed. Or rather, it would be in a little over an hour's time.

'You're joking, right?'

'No. Not when it comes to The Jam.'

'No, I didn't think you were. What does it look like? Have you managed to get a look at it yet?'

'No, man. It's been off limits. I haven't seen the sleeve. I don't think I can wait till nine, you know.'

'Me neither. Let's play ping-pong. You never know, it might just distract us . . .'

Ping-pong didn't distract us, not even when we decided to elevate it from ping-pong to table tennis. I'd drunk so much Coke in the last sixty minutes that each one of my teeth felt as if it was wearing its very own pair of hand-knitted, woolly winter socks.

Suddenly, the lights went out and we were plunged into almost complete darkness. I could just about make out a shape on its way up to the booth. 'Look – I think Nick's going to play "Underground" . . .'

Anyone could DJ at Youthy. All you had to do was put your name down on the waiting list. It normally didn't take too long for your turn to come around because you couldn't DJ for the whole night, you had to share the record booth with two others and so this meant that each of you got about three-quarters of an hour each.

Nick weaved his way through the dance floor, stepped up into the booth and closed the door behind him. Dust and a plume of blue smoke caught in the light from the single, small spotlight on the ceiling which lit up the turntable, like a lighthouse beam going round and round.

The needle dropped down onto the seven black inches of glistening vinyl, the amp picked up the short, sharp crackle and everything was in slow motion and next came a great, thumpy cluster of bars of bass from Bruce to start with and then, seconds later, Paul's Rickenbacker came crashing in from nowhere and then here came the vocal. I'd heard only ten seconds of this song and already, deep down inside me, I knew that my life had undergone some sort of transformation. The song felt like an anthem. This was the most perfect sound I'd ever heard in my life. It was urgent and jumpy and when Paul's lyrics came, they almost spat out of the speakers and whilst everyone else was dancing I was just left standing there in the middle of the dance floor.

I thought that I knew enough about Paul to know that there had to be some hidden meaning in there, but for the moment all I cared about was how it made me feel. It made me feel like I was on fire inside. As soon as it started it was over, as quick as a flash, just like that. There was some heavy reverb at the end and then, nothing, just static as the needle rode the play-out groove.

I turned and looked at Rik, who'd been leaping around throughout, playing air guitar. He nodded at me, 'Not bad, Dave. Not half bad at all, mate.' Dear Richard, the master of all that is understated. I wanted to tell him what I'd just felt, what it was that I was feeling, about how I'd been touched by this beautiful, powerful song that Paul had so lovingly crafted, about how, somehow, everything was different for me then and always would be. I wanted to tell him that for me, things had changed. I could not. Instead, I settled for, 'Yep. I quite liked it.' It was then that I realised what was odd about Rik. His top lip – there were the beginnings of a moustache on it. How could I have missed it?

'What are you staring at, Dave?'

'Nothing . . .'

I could see Nick Wright over in the corner, his back against the wall. He was snogging some girl who looked like one of Legs & Co. Then some greasy biker type shuffled into the booth with an armful of battered LPs under his arm and selected a track: Rainbow's 'Since You've Been Gone' – one of my all time most hated songs. Bloody Rainbow – they looked like a bunch of clowns living rough.

I watched him take Nick's single off the turntable, slip it back inside its sleeve and put it on the side of the mixing desk, propped up against the window of the booth next to the door. I looked back at Nick who was still snogging the girl. Both of his eyes were closed and one of his hands was on her bottom. Did some lucky guy have his hand on Fiona's bottom right then? I was still smarting from how stupid I'd been with Fi a week ago. The biker creature rummaged around inside the pockets of his sleeveless denim jacket which he was wearing over his disgusting old leathers, patting them till he finally found his fags. He took out a packet of Marlboro, lit one and walked over to the double doors, opened them and stood in the doorway blowing his smoke out into the night air, gently headbanging along to his bloody Rainbow. And then it hit me, my song was right there, just waiting for me. If only I could find the balls . . .

I was one hundred per cent certain that if I did this and got caught, then my life would not be worth living. But I simply could not help myself. The urge had swollen up inside me and I could feel it squirming around my stomach, gnawing away at my insides telling me not to wait, that I could not wait, that waiting was absolutely the wrong thing to do. I fully appreciated the risk if I was caught, and the inevitable kicking of a lifetime if I was discovered, but I was The Only Jam Fan Worthy Of This – it would be mine. Oh yes, it would be mine . . .

I was aware of Rik watching me from the other side of the room, and I had one eye on the heavy and one eye on Nick. I sauntered up to the booth, reached out my hand and then, in an instant, his copy of 'Going Underground' was inside my blazer and tucked away under my arm. It was a dream, I told myself that I wasn't really doing it and before I knew it I was out through the doors, past the foul biker and was almost halfway home before I finally stopped running.

Up in my room I sat on the end of my bed staring at the picture of The Jam on the front of the record sleeve. They were on a television screen staring back at me. Paul was wearing a black and white polka dot cravat, tied loosely like a scarf over a smart black jacket. Had he read my poem yet? I hadn't told Rik that I'd written to Paul, he'd probably extract the piss so much it just wasn't worth telling him. Anyway, I liked the thought of Paul and I sharing our own little special secret. Rick wore a blazer far too stripy to save him from looking like he should be selling ice cream instead of drumming in The Jam – he'd got his arms folded and looked cross. I didn't blame him, I'd be furious if I was wearing that thing. Bruce was wearing a jumper – but he didn't seem to mind. He looked like he'd just come in from doing something in the garden, maybe creosoting his fence.

I played the record, transfixed by its brilliance. I took

it off the turntable, turned it over and played the other side, 'The Dreams Of Children'. Another special song, with some backwards guitar at the start which I instantly recognised as something off *Setting Sons* but couldn't pin down as I was so wired from committing the crime of stealing Nick Wright's record. These were two more perfect Jam songs. Two double A-sides. How did Paul know so much about me that he wrote songs so special to me? Did he sneak into my room late at night whilst I was asleep and peep inside my head? He must do.

I carefully placed the single back in its sleeve and then hid it under my pants inside my chest of drawers. I got undressed, put on my pyjamas, washed my face and cleaned my teeth. I felt so guilty I could barely look at myself in the bathroom mirror. What a prat, stealing another Jam fan's record. How would I feel if some idiot did that to me?

I went downstairs to make myself a cup of tea. The horror of what would happen to me if Nick Wright found out who stole his record was driving me mad. My hand trembled as I squeezed the back of the bag on the inside of the cup and the spoon rattled against the china. The phone in the hall rang. 'I'll get it.' I picked up the receiver on the Trimphone.

'Hello?' Jesus Christ. It was Rik – I must have been rumbled! He was calling to tell me that Nick now knew that it was me who stole it, and that he was on his way round now to kick my stupid, stupid head inside out. Oh, help. Oh, someone please help me. Jesus, please help me, Paul! Don't be stupid, David, I told myself. There's no way he could know it was me. My imagination was running away with itself. Get a grip, man.

'Hello? Dave?' Not good. He sounds worried. This was bad.

'Yeah, what's up?'

'Just wondering where you sloped off to?'

See, it's nothing – stop panicking, Linesy. 'Sorry, Rik. Just remembered I'd got some English homework to finish off. I tried to find you to say cheerio, but you weren't anywhere around, man.'

'Oh, right. It's just that I thought I'd best give you a quick ring.'

'Why? Are you still at Youthy?'

'Yeah, but Nick Wright's not. In fact, he's on his scooter right this very minute and he's on his way round to your house. I reckon he'll be there in less than ten minutes . . .'

It was official. My life as I knew it was now over. 'What?'

'It's true – and he's so pissed off you wouldn't believe it.' I could hear the music in the background at Youthy, those clowns The Village People. Maybe I could run away to the Navy.

'How does he know where I live?'

'He flushed my head down the loo to get your address out of me.'

'Jesus. He flushed your head down the loo?'

'Well, he didn't actually flush my head down the loo, but he said he would if I didn't tell him.'

'Cheers, Rik – you're a real mate.'

'Don't mention it.'

'Rik, I'm scared.'

'And so you should be, he's bringing a pool cue. Looked like a Knight of the Round fucking Table as he set off on his Lambretta with that thing under his arm.'

I was dead. I might as well be dead right then. My life, from that point on, was going to be one great, big, living nightmare. Oh, no – I heard an engine outside the house. I could hardly hear Rik down the phone, banging on about could he have my record collection if I died, but I could make out every other word because of all the blood that was churning away inside my head. I felt like I might be about to wet myself. 'Hello? Dave? Hello? Are you still there?'

Outside, I heard the kickstand of Nick's scooter going down. Then the engine stopped. I thought that my heart might stop, too.

'Yeah, I'm still here. Just. Look, I'm going to have to go now. I really need the loo.'

'Don't go. You'll be fine, I promise you.'

'Man alive, how am I gonna be fine? I'm about to get the whotsits battered out of me by the hardest, biggest, angriest mod in Garforth and you know what? I don't fucking blame him. Not one bit do I blame him.'

There were footsteps on the drive and somebody at the front door. Oh. My. God. The knocker took an urgent hammering and I could see his shape through the smoked glass panel. He moved around, hopping from foot to foot. This man was literally hopping mad. I silently slipped the brass safety chain across the door. Maybe I could get Chris or Phil to answer it and just tell him that I'm out? Or maybe I could get Mum or Dad to tell him that I've gone to bed early? No, none of these things were going to work – I had to take this like a man. Now, think David. What would Paul do? WHAT WOULD PAUL DO? Paul wouldn't need to do anything to get out of this mess because he wouldn't have been such an idiot in the first place, you idiot.

The knocker went again and this time it sounded like gunfire going off in the porch. I thought he must have been using the pool cue to try and batter down the door. I didn't think I could hold this piss inside me for much longer. 'Not my face,' I said out loud to myself, 'anything, just please don't hit me in my face.' Slowly, very slowly, I lifted the latch and eased the door open just an inch. The security chain would let it open twice as far, but that was enough for the moment. Maybe I could run upstairs and get the record, and if I just handed it to him, slipped it through the gap and said sorry, then that whole terrible, terrifying business would go away. Don't be ridiculous, David – Nick Wright wasn't just there for his record, he wanted his pound of flesh to go with it. I could hear Rik down the phone screaming, 'Dave, Dave, what's that noise? Are you OK?'

I removed the security chain and took a deep, deep breath. My lungs hurt when I breathed in. My head hurt and I was about to be left standing in a puddle of my own pee. I didn't put the phone back on its cradle because it was the only available weapon which I'd got to hand. I raised it above my head ready to bring down on the bridge of Nick's nose. The element of surprise might just work in my favour – the last thing he'd be expecting was a turquoise Trimphone coming at him.

I took a step back, opened the front door and found myself face to face with Mr Jones, the pools collector. 'Now then, son. It's two weeks' money tonight because me and the wife are off to her sister's in Filey. Have you got your dad's coupons ready?' All I could do was look at him. I couldn't even speak. Rik had obviously heard the whole thing. I could hear him laughing hysterically down the phone. He sounded like he was wetting *him*self. I lifted the receiver to my ear. He was trying to splutter something out but was laughing too hard to be intelligible. I said nothing. I just put the phone down and walked slowly upstairs to the bathroom. The relief poured out of me, straight into the loo. Mr Jones nearly got more pools than he was looking for that night. Rik's unwitting accomplice had made his wind-up complete.

One week later The Jam were at number one with 'Going Underground' and 'The Dreams Of Children' as a double A-side. They were the first band for seven years to go straight to the top of the charts. The last group to do this was Slade, back in 1973. I was watching them perform it on *Top Of The Pops* – just for me. Paul wore an apron especially for the occasion. He'd turned it the other way around so he couldn't be accused of advertising Heinz tomato soup and I thought he was wearing it because he wanted us all to know that even though he was at number one, nothing would change him and he was still a normal person who loved everyday things and wouldn't change because of success. That's how I saw it, anyway.

I could barely bring myself to watch because I'd been sucker-punched in the face by the fact that I was a thief. I really shouldn't have been allowed to watch this, because I stole another man's copy of 'Going Underground'. I wouldn't be responsible for their success unless I went out and bought a copy. I made a promise to Paul that the next day I'd go out and buy two copies, to try and make amends.

Rik's mum and dad had bought a brand new video recorder and Rik'd even got his own video cassette. We'd decided to make our very own Jam tape that'd be our private copy full of stuff that they do on the telly, and that *TOTP* performance would be our first clip. What a one to start with! I called Rik up to see if he'd finished his tea (they ate late, the Bowermans) so I could go round there to watch it again. 'It's me. Did you see them?'

'No. We were eating, so I set the tape. We can watch it together in a bit if you want. Was it skill?'

'Yeah, it was skill. Paul wore an apron.'

'He wore an apron? What for?'

'I reckon it was because he wanted to say to everyone that success hasn't changed him and he still does the dishes despite being at number one.'

'Oh. I'm stacking everything into the dishwasher right now.' The Bowermans had a phone, in their kitchen, on the wall, like the one in *Diff'rent Strokes* with a really long, massive flex that stretched to wherever you were in the kitchen.

'Yeah, it was a bright red apron with "Heinz Tomato Soup" on it, but he'd turned it round so you couldn't see it. Probably something to do with the BBC and advertising or something like that.'

Rik sounded excited. 'A Heinz tomato soup apron? Paul was wearing one of those on *Top Of The Pops*?'

'That's right. And he made it look kind of cool.'

'I don't believe it.'

'You'd better believe it.'

'No, I believe it, Dave, it's just that my mum's got one of those somewhere. I'll try and hunt it out – I can wear it at Youthy next week. See you in half an hour . . .'

Bastard. Complete and utter total bastard.

Thirty minutes later I was sitting on Rik's sofa in front of the telly. I say in front of the telly, it seemed like roughly a mile and a half away. Their living room was massive, just like the rest of the house. The sofa was so far away from the television the remote control didn't function properly and Rik had to stand on one leg and lean forwards with his arm outstretched like some sort of mad ballerina to try and make it work. I could have done with a pair of binoculars to see the screen and he was wearing his mum's apron. Bastard.

'Do you like it?'

'It's all right,' I said.

Rik smoothed the plastic apron down, took a swig from his can of Fanta and turned the video recorder on. He sat back down and started fiddling with the remote.

'Where did your Mum get it from, then?'

'Radio Rentals, in Main Street. We've got it on a month's trial. Dad says that if we like it, we'll buy it, because by the time we've had it for a year we may as well have just paid for it, given what it costs to rent the thing. It's a Betamax. They're the best. I might ask for one of these for my bedroom for Christmas . . .'

'No, man, the apron. Where did she get the *apron* from?'

'Dunno. But I'll ask her if you want.'

'Cheers.' I sat back and sucked on the straw in my carton of Five Alive, getting myself ready to watch Paul again. I hated Rik for having that apron, but I hated myself more for feeling so petty and jealous. How could I be jealous of Rik having an apron? Easy – because it was just like Paul's.

'Right. I'll rewind the tape. They shouldn't be too far back seeing that they were on last. Then we can work out which pictures we want to cut out and stick on the front of the video cassette box. Have you thought about what you might want on there?'

The video began winding back and Rik did his pointy ballet thing and then the machine juddered to a halt. 'Kind of. I thought that the "Going Underground" sleeve would be a good pic, because they're, you know, on the television screen on the front of the single sleeve and this compilation tape's all about them being on television. So, whatcha think?'

'Good idea. Hold onto you hat – here we go . . .'

Rik pressed nine on the remote and the screen went blue. Then he pressed the play button on the handset and here came The Jam. Only, it wasn't The Jam at all. It was Seth fucking Armstrong complaining about losing his ferret down Annie Sugden's back warren. 'You've taped the wrong side, you utter ponce.'

'It wasn't me who set the tape, it was my dad.'

'Well, he's a ponce as well as you.'

'Why does that make me a ponce?'

'Because you should have checked it, you ponce. You can't go leaving serious, responsible matters such as this to unreliable people like parents. They can't be trusted with tasks levelled at this high a priority, you should know that. What happens if they're not number one this time next week? We'll have lost this classic clip forever, you great ponce.'

'Stop calling me a ponce.'

'No. This is one almighty cock-up, Rik.'

'Sorry. Really sorry. How can I make it up to you?'

Beat.

'Give us your apron, you ponce.'

I didn't know it at the time, but the reason behind Paul's apron was to illustrate his growing interest in pop art. This certainly pissed off the people at the BBC, who shat themselves at any hint of an artiste endorsing a product of any description.

Paul Weller wasn't setting out to endorse a product. What he was doing was using the apron as a reference to The Who's album, *The Who Sell Out*. It featured Roger Daltrey grasping a huge tin of Heinz baked beans, and PW was taking the piss, having a laugh, because he anticipated the reaction from the likes of the *NME* to his band's new-found success; that The Jam, by being number one, had finally sold out for good.

It transpired that the suits at the Beeb decided that Paul should not be granted free rein to don the Heinz apron. No way. Paul, typically, dug his Italian heels in and agreed to play only if he could wear it reversed. They relented, and the camera lights lit it up like a Christmas tree, the logo as clear as day for all to clock. Paul won. Despite this, he felt used and abused by those in power at Television Centre and deliberately cocked his lines up. The end result was seriously amateurish.

'Going Underground' wasn't about taking a tube ride. It was about Russia invading Afghanistan in December 1979. It's the story of a working man, told by the government to play along, pay for the war and not to complain whilst doing so. The next week at Youthy there were squaddies from the local barracks jumping up and down, singing away to the lyrics. It was obvious to me that they had no idea what they were singing along to. I pitied them as I watched them dance around in their combat green and polished boots.

What many don't know, is that 'Going Underground' became a double A-side with 'The Dreams Of Children' on the flip as the result of a basic mistake.

Paul, Bruce and Rick had slated 'The Dreams Of Children' as a future A-side. The record was printed in France, and a typo resulted in an A replacing the B; the result – a double A-side. 'Going Underground' was more in keeping with the regular 'Jam sound', so the radio programmers concentrated on playing that. The crucial point here, is that at last, Polydor were now one hundred per cent into The Jam and purposefully delayed the record's release by seven days – which meant that they gave themselves seven more days of big sales in the form of advance orders from fans.

The way that Polydor distributed meant that The Jam were kept at the top slot for three weeks on the trot. So far that year, no band had stayed there longer. It was a record only bettered by The Police, in October, with 'Don't Stand So Close To Me'. Which was bollocks. Polydor threw their corporate hat into the ring. They released every Jam single all at once. The demand was enormous, with sales resulting in six of their singles all making the charts at once – 'In The City' went in at forty, 'All Around The World' at forty-three, 'Strange Town' at forty-four, 'The Modern World' at fifty-two, 'News of the World' at fifty-three and 'David Watts' at fifty-four. This was the single most successful assault on the charts any group had had since The Beatles. And I'd helped put them back there. I bought two 'Undergrounds' and one of each single to get the picture sleeves. Long live The Jam!

5

Start!

With the summer came this absolute scorcher from the mighty pen of Paul. I'd spent the last twenty weeks waiting by the front door for a reply from Riot Stories about my poem, but I could see why it would take Paul so long to find the time to write – it must have taken him forever to come up with something as good as 'Start!'. 'Start!' is just the most amazingly original sound for a song to have. It sounds . . . like a merry-go-round descending down a hill into madness having just spun off its axis. The frustration and anger in PW's voice leaps off the record, it infected and enthused me, although I'd no idea what on earth he was singing about. It's got horns on it, and they screeched out like the swifts which nested under our eaves. I'd just seen the video on *Top Of The Pops* and in it Paul wore a pair of dark sunglasses shaped just like John Lennon's spectacles. I mentioned this to Mum.

'That's exactly why he's wearing them.'

I put down my bottle of orange Soda Stream and gave her a look which said 'What do you know about it? You're a parent. Now please stop trying to meddle in matters which don't concern you and get back to your world, thank you very much . . .'

'That's why he's wearing those Lennon glasses – because this record sounds just like a Beatles song. It's his way of saying thanks to The Beatles.'

What on earth was she talking about? 'Hmm . . . I'll take your word for it.' I got back to my Soda Stream. I'd give Rik a ring in a bit to make sure he hadn't made a bummer on the Jam tape again. Beatles song? I ask you!

During that summer I'd written some more brilliant poems for Paul and Mum had been kind enough to photocopy them at the hospital where she'd got a new job as a secretary. It was good of her to do it, but it was painful handing over my personal, private poetry to my mum. They were vivid, clear insights into my own little secret world and I wondered who was most embarrassed – me, knowing that Mum had read them, or Mum actually reading them?

By then, Mum had been at the hospital for three weeks. She said that she took the job to help her meet new people and hopefully make some new friends and generally just to get out and about a bit more. She liked it, I could tell. It certainly suited her. She whistled to herself in the morning on the way to catch the bus and she'd started doing her hair differently. She had professional hair.

Mum said that the poetry photocopying wasn't a problem, but that I shouldn't bother asking her to type any of it up, because she hadn't got a typewriter – she'd got something 'truly evil' called a word processor. She said that she despaired of it, and that using it was 'like learning how to fly a bloody passenger jet. Where's the ruddy ribbon go? If someone would show me where the ribbon goes, the rest'd fall into place . . .' Apparently, they were sending her on a course.

Dad wasn't around much at the time. He'd been up

and down the country seeing clients, attending seminars, sales conferences, that sort of thing. We all missed him, and Chris and Phil seemed to more than me; they didn't have Paul to fall back on, and despite having settled in quicker and more easily than me at first, having new mates to the house for tea and stuff like that, they still needed their dad – just like me, but they seemed to need him a little bit more. And he knew it. It could have been worse, much worse, Dad could have been stuck out in the middle of the North Sea or abroad or banged up in prison or just not around at all. Mum was happier now that she'd got her job to distract her, and all in all the machinery of the house seemed to have oiled itself well enough to operate smoothly.

Apart from writing my poetry I'd also spent much of my time incredibly busy trying very hard not to grow a moustache. It was seriously hard work. All of the filthy bikers and heavies loved their hair on their lips. Me, I really hated it. Some of them in the upper sixth even had beards. Imagine that – being at school with a bloody beard! What was next – patches on the elbows and a pipe on the go? The moustache wasn't for me . . . certainly not; I was a mod – not a maths teacher. So, I'd been keeping the thing at bay with Dad's trusty old cut-throat razor. After my first, hideous attempt at using it on my head, I'd learned my lesson. Dad said he'd teach me to shave properly when there was enough hair on my lip and chin to have a good go at. I hoped I'd make a better go of it than I'd done with the hair on my head.

As well as writing poetry and not growing a moustache, I'd been hanging around with Rik after school, getting royally thrashed by him at snooker (our one concession to the sunshine was to move his table out onto his parents' lawn: not ideal when a rain cloud would surprise us – probably one of the few times when rain stopped play in a snooker match). We also went for long bike rides which I thoroughly enjoyed, despite Rik's racer weighing less than my saddlebag which meant that I had to pedal four times as much just to keep up with him. I didn't mind: I was developing calf muscles which looked like legs of lamb. I was happy and healthy and I loved to explore the surrounding villages on my BSA tourer. We'd cycle to Barwick-in-Elmet and sit under the maypole drinking lemon barley water from our flasks. They were happy days.

* * *

Recently, there'd been a bit of trouble in Bridgford, and that was one of the reasons why Grampa came to stay. He'd been phoning up most nights and none of us could make out what he was going on about. Grampa had my room and I was going to be on the zed bed thingy, in Chris and Phil's room. The first thing that Grampa did when he arrived was to take out a bottle of Scotch from his handbag, pour himself a glass, light a gigantic cigar and ask if there were any wildlife documentaries on the telly. 'I like wildlife, Davey. And *Juliet Bravo* . . .'

Chris had got a Rubik's cube and he took the thing everywhere. It was like it was glued to him, never leaving his soft, pudgy hands. Even when he was in another room, I could tell where he was in the house just by listening for the telltale click-clack, shlick-shlack of the cube as he forever twisted and turned the thing, trying to crack the combination and fall upon the answer.

I watched him through the fug of Grampa's cigar. We were all sitting round the telly watching *Juliet Bravo*. Chris was watching the box, but his mind was on the cube, whirring the columns round and around. He was doing it without knowing, and even if Chris did crack the cube, he probably wouldn't even have noticed. Later that night, when we were all in bed, I fell asleep to the sound of Chris and his cube. I wondered if he did it in his sleep. Chris had started wearing Kickers on his feet – they were favoured by French exchange students and geography teachers and to tell you the truth, even though they weren't standard mod issue, I quite liked them. I'd never have worn a pair, though. Not unless Paul did.

On the news before bed there was a piece about an amazing new revolution in music. It was called a compact disc and was known as a CD. They were very new and set to become massive in America and you could get hundreds of songs onto one little silver disc which was smaller than a single. Paul wouldn't need those CD things – The Jam didn't sell well in the United States. I decided at that moment never to set foot in the cursed country as at the time it was clearly a place not worth visiting. It must be rubbish if they didn't dig The Jam. I didn't dig the idea of the CD, either. They looked antiseptic. 'Who'd have thought it, eh?' I looked at Grampa, slumped in the armchair, ash all down his cardigan, scanning the carpet for something.

'It's incredible, isn't it, Gramps,' I said, pointing at the television. Anything to make conversation.

'You can say that again. I could have sworn I had a bottle down here . . .'

From the kitchen, I could hear Dad pouring the rest of it down the sink.

At breakfast the next day, Grampa put his cigar out in the empty shell of his boiled egg and asked me, 'Them posters up on your wall, do you like those Jam people, do you?'

I swallowed a mouthful of toast and replied, 'Yeah, Grampa, I like those people.'

'You've done your hair the same way as the lanky one.' Here we go. 'I said, you've got the same hair as the lanky one.'

Quick sip of tea and a nice smile was the only reply Grampa was getting on that one.

'You used to have such lovely hair till you moved up here. Wavy Davey, that's what we used to call you. Wavy Davey.'

I felt like my head was going to explode. 'More tea, Grampa?'

'You never used to part it down the middle. It used to be a side parting, it used to be a man's parting. You won't get your hair cut like that in my barber's shop, not now or ever . . .'

I struggled to find a suitably acidic reply, but unfortunately my caustic cupboard was entirely bare. Thankfully, Mum changed the subject.

'Jess, let me take you down the garden and show you my camellia.'

Grampa Lines had the most amazing life, but despite this, each time that he visited or we went and saw him in Bridgford, there was never anything that I felt I could actually *say* to him. I wanted to ask Grampa about how he served as a fireman during the war, stationed on the South Coast, about the boats ablaze from the bombs which rained down on the harbour, night after night. I wanted to ask Grampa about all sorts of family things, like just why was it that Slack Alice never came down for tea with us when we visited and instead had cake left outside her door? What happened when his partner in their song and dance routine got hit by a tram and died? Couldn't he find another partner to team up with, or had that done it for him? What was it like to come from completely nowhere and end up being the best and most famous barber in the Midlands? What was it like when Granny died and how did he feel being left alone in the house with that scary mangle in the wash house? I wanted to ask him if there really was a Black

Hand that lived in the little orchard at the bottom of the garden which scratched the trunk of the tree where we sometimes sat in the sunshine. Did he think he might meet Granny again when he died? Did he wear his slippers when he went out to the shop for cigars?

I sat on the sofa and thought about these questions. These were the sort of personal things that I could easily have asked Grampa Sewter about, all day, every day. Until we moved to Leeds, that is. Ten minutes later Mum and Grampa came in from the garden.

'David, I'm making coffee. Would you like a cup?'

'Yes please, Mum.'

'Good. We can all sit down and have a nice little chat whilst your Dad fills the car up before he takes Grampa back to Bridgford. You sit with your gramps while I put the kettle on. You never know, I might even conjure up some Blue Ribbands from somewhere.'

Grampa sat down next to me on the sofa. He leaned back and put his arm around me, pulling me towards him in an all-lads-together kind of way. 'Now then, Davey boy. What have you got to tell your old Grampa?' I couldn't see him. He'd got a Havana on the go and I looked at a big, blue cloud which was suspended above the sofa. The cloud cleared, and Grampa Lines emerged from it, blinking out at me from behind the lenses of his spectacles. I thought about what I could possibly tell this man. I could have told him about my poetry, my new friends at school, how I'd got some new hay-fever pills and how they weren't bad at all but that they made me feel drowsy. I could tell Grampa about how much I still missed Bridgford, with its avenues lined with cherry blossom, and even though I was settled in Leeds it would always be my real home. I thought of telling him about kissing Fiona on the cricket pitch and I wondered about asking for tips on cutting my own hair. I thought of all of those things, and then I said, 'I think there's a programme on, all about giraffes.'

'That'll do nicely, Davey Boy.'

Half an hour later Chris, Phil and Mum and I were standing in the front garden,waving goodbye to Grampa. Sitting next to Dad in the front passenger seat, Grampa looked tiny. I watched him open his handbag and take out a plastic Barclay's bank bag, the sort you keep coins in. Because Grampa dealt in cash at the barber's shop, this is what he'd got used to carrying his money around in all the time. He didn't have a wallet; what he had was a different bag for each coin and each note. He took the twenty pound note bag out, peeled one off and placed it on the dashboard for petrol money. He'd always done the same whenever Dad took him anywhere, but none of us had the heart to tell him that Dad claimed back the petrol on expenses. Dad took the money, put it into his pocket and the dark brown Austin Maxi slipped quietly away.

I went straight to my room because I could feel a poem coming on. It'd been a little while since I'd felt the urge to write anything, so this came as a nice surprise. I got my pen out in readiness. After more than an hour I hadn't made one single, solitary mark on the page. No words would come, no poem, no lines to rhyme. This was the best possible news in the world! I was overjoyed by it – I was a real, living, breathing writer. How could I not be when I was quite clearly suffering from writer's block? I celebrated by having a sly smoke out of the bedroom window whilst listening to Paul singing words so soulful and sweet. Afterwards, I laid back on my bed and drifted off, like the smoke in the summer's breeze.

I awoke after a couple of hours, got up and straightened my bed. There was a weird silence in the house that I could only put down to Grampa going which was odd because he never made any noise when he was there. Maybe it was just me, but I somehow got the feeling that he wasn't coming back. I shook out the duvet, and there, fluttering from inside, was a piece of square, silk cloth. It was golden, with a claret paisley print and was exactly the sort of thing that Paul would have worn, an item of great style and fine beauty, and I wanted it for myself. He wouldn't mind if I borrowed it till next time I saw him. I tied it around my neck and stood in front of the mirror. It looked superb, and became a highly original addition to my modernist wardrobe. The first time Rik saw me wearing it, I swear that he actually went a deep, dark shade of jealous jade.

The next day, I came home from school and as I turned the corner I saw Dad's car parked in the drive. This was unheard of. Not only was he supposed to be in Cardiff, it had only just gone four in the afternoon. Dad was never at home at four in the afternoon. There was more chance of me coming home and finding the batmobile in our drive.

Dad sat in the garden, perched on the little low wall between the patio and the clipped lawn. He was smoking a cigarette and playing with his hair. He looked older, he looked like his dad. Mum was sitting next to him, and next to Dad this made her appear much younger. Her face was fresh and her freckles were having a field day. She looked like she could be in the sixth form at school.

'It's over.'

I looked at Dad and now his face was ashen. His face was thin, in an instant, his face was thinner.

'What's over?'

He bit his thin, wide bottom lip and there were tiny pools of tears in his eyes. His trouser leg had risen up and I noticed that his bony ankles matched his sharp cheekbones.

'Grampa Lines died today. The warden found him, they called an ambulance but by the time it got there he'd gone, it was too late. I never should have left him in Nottingham.' Dad whispered this last sentence and I looked at Mum and she looked at me as if neither of us were meant to hear it.

I wanted to ask if it was something specific that killed him, or just old age. I wanted to ask Dad if it was the endless Scotch, the constant cigars or loneliness? But I didn't, because I saw how upset he was. He didn't deserve that sort of questioning, he'd done the best thing for all of us, moving the family up here. It wasn't my father who undid the necks on those hundreds of bottles of Scotch, it wasn't him who poured them down Grampa's throat every night. My dad brought us to Leeds so that we could have a better life and the blame, if that's the right word, rested solely with Grampa. Grampa had been here the day before and now he would never come here again. It was deeply weird to think that. I was upset, but I was upset for my dad. Both of his parents were now dead and his ties with Bridgford buried with them. I truly felt for him.

Later that night, I was in my room listening to the last Jam tape Rik and I had made. It'd got lots of slow songs and it suited my mood. There was a brief knock on the door and Dad opened it, popped his head round and asked if he could come in. I almost fell over in shock. Normally, he came through it like he was in *The Sweeney*. He sat down and gave me a hug and I hugged him back and there was just a moment when we looked each other in the eye and even though we said nothing, we said everything. Dad had bought me my first razor and he'd come up to give it to me. I stared at the slim, silvery-handled instrument and ran my finger length-ways across the twin blades.

'Be careful, son – you'll cut yourself.' He handed

me a can of shaving foam and said, 'I didn't think it was wise you trying to use the cut-throat, not yet. Not after what you did to your head.'

I laughed, and agreed with him. 'Thanks. It feels weird owning one of these.'

Dad nodded, 'Well, you're growing up. You'd better get used to it.'

He led me to the bathroom and filled the sink. I rinsed my face and Dad dabbed the foam over it for me. He took the razor from my hand. 'Here, let me show you, son.'

The following Wednesday was Grampa Lines's funeral. It had been decided that Phil was too young to attend, and, because Chris had flu, I should stay at home and look after them. It wouldn't have felt right going to school anyway. I would have wanted to be at the funeral. Instead, I made scrambled eggs on toast for tea for the three of us. I would have liked to have gone, to say goodbye, but as it was always hard enough saying hello to Grampa, I didn't feel too bad. I don't think that Dad would have appreciated me seeing him upset. Anyway, I liked playing at being Big Brother – maybe I should have tried it more often. I wore the cravat around the house that day – it was my way of saying goodbye. I felt like I was wearing a paisley flag, at half mast.

It was a while before I came to discover just what 'Start!' was really about. It was Paul's interpretation of George Orwell's book, *Homage To Catalonia*. In it, Orwell wrote about how he fought against fascism during the Spanish Civil War. Orwell documented how he, and many other people who shared his own ideals of democratic socialism, travelled to Barcelona to fight for what they thought was right. They came from all over the globe, and even though the first man did not know what the second was saying in their mother tongues, if they could get through for just two minutes then it would be a . . . Start! When I hear it now, it reminds me about how much I'd have loved to communicate, to get through to Grampa.

6

Absolute Beginners

It was October, 1981, and my fifteenth birthday was four months away. It was more than a year since Grampa died and I was surprised that the time had gone so quickly. It was the first time for me that death became a date to remember.

Mum had been on and on at me to 'get stuck in more' at school. I had been toying with the idea of joining an after-school society and I felt a definite pull towards drama. There was a drama club which met every Thursday after school and I'd been six or seven times. I couldn't tell you if I'd enjoyed it or not because

I'd never actually been in. I was too intimidated to walk in and introduce myself: I just watched through the glass panel in the door.

I'd embraced being a mod, but, like Paul, I'd grown out of the mob culture that went with it. For me, modernism wasn't so much about being part of the mod movement, it was becoming increasingly more about my connection to Paul. If 1980 was a peak for Weller, then he thought 1981 was a filthy, lousy trough. Paul said as much in an interview, that it had 'been a horrible year for songs'. I disagree – 'Absolute Beginners' is one of The Jam's cleanest, crispest, most enduring tunes. It's bitter, like chewing lemons, and it's full of hope and incredibly revealing all at the same time. It has an almighty kick to it, an urgency fuelled by the horn section who play short, sharp, stabbing notes which drive it along, lifting the melody and adding weight and substance. This song sounded to me like a new chapter – it's classic Jam and even today, never far from my turntable: it was released on 16 October, 1981, and reached number four in the charts.

'Absolute Beginners' – what a song title; where did it come from? What was the story? I sat down and read an article in *Sounds* which credited the title to a book by a writer whom I'd never heard. His name was Colin MacInnes, and I set out my stall to find out just who he was. It didn't take me long. MacInnes wrote the theme tune to 'Being Young' long before anyone else did. I ordered a copy of *Absolute Beginners* from the library and when it arrived, I devoured it in one sitting. I *ate* the book up.

MacInnes wrote with the keenest, brightest of eyes. His take on Being Young is inspired, and I wondered how old he was, how many summers he had under his belt when he set pen to paper. Despite it being set in the sixties it was written in the fifties, so what this man did was chronicle the most famous English decade even before it had actually begun. He wrote books like Paul Weller wrote lyrics – from the heart.

Absolute Beginners blew my mind. MacInnes wrote about the path of boyhood and its journey into manhood like his own footsteps were still wet and sticky in the sand, warm from the sun between his toes and hot and humid from the London tarmac on the soles of his handmade, shining Italian loafers. The hero has no name; his profession: photographer. He neither drinks nor smokes, preferring the buzz of simply being cool to that provided by artificial stimulants. He moves within certain circles, clocking the characters and taking them in, rarely passing judgement, simply making mental notes and moving on. When I read *Absolute Beginners* I had to listen to the song of the same name at the same time – the two went hand in hand, they complemented and enhanced each other. Paul had set this coming-of-age novel to music, and I danced through the pages to his tune. It made me feel like maybe becoming a man wasn't such a hard slog after all; that by being true to myself, I might just get there. That is until one day when the act of growing up took a rather embarrassing turn.

I was walking home from school at the end of the day, down the old railway track, and I'd just made a promise to myself that this was the last time I'd ever take this route because I was completely and utterly pissed off at getting mud splashes all up my trousers and crap caked all over my shoes – very unmod indeed.

It was a little blustery and the empty, colourful crisp packets dressed the hawthorn like bunting on a car lot. I passed an abandoned pram rusting under a hedgerow and spied a baby, made of moulded plastic, its head sticking out from under one wheel. The wind rustled its hair and its eyes stared out at me and for just a moment, I could swear that it said 'Help me'. It was disgusting, all this litter everywhere, yet I was drawn to the baby doll. I wanted to help it. It was a thoroughly ridiculous feeling, but it was an urge that I was unable to control. The crappy litter, the discarded, dumped rubbish was enough, but the plastic baby, that had to be tidied away – I couldn't leave it there, it sickened me so. The least I could do was to put it in the black bin liner full of newspapers that had been left next to it.

I tramped through the brambles, careful not to snag my tonic Sta-Prest trousers – this was dangerous territory for clothes, and I was ultra-careful on my way in, flattening down any potentially evil bits with my haversack before moving further on. I picked up the baby and went to drop it into the bin liner and there, staring up at me from inside the bag, was the most gorgeous woman I'd ever set eyes on in my whole life.

She was blonde, with long, thick curls as golden as a wheat field in the midday sunshine and she was spread over the centrefold of a porn mag. Her eyes were heavily made-up and her beautiful face had the filthiest feel about it, she looked directly into the camera and she'd got the most brilliant breasts, not like anyone at school, full and round and barely stuffed into a black, lace bra. I whipped out the magazine and crammed it into my haversack, flung the baby in the bag and hotfooted it home sharpish.

After cheese on toast for tea I retired to my room making the excuse that I had to deal with homework. I could hardly manage to swallow a mouthful because I was so excited at the thought of being left alone with the model in the mag. I shut the bedroom door and got her out. Her body was so smooth, and her long, graceful legs went on and on and on. She was perfect in every way. Her name was Melissa, she was twenty-three years old and, according to the magazine, was currently without a boyfriend. I quickly turned the page, and when I saw what she was doing next, I could hardly contain myself. She only had on the most gloriously sexy pair of . . . shoes. Black, velvet, strappy high heels with little ribbons which tied around her ankles; her little toenails painted pink peeped out from the front. It was almost too much for me. I tore off my trousers and stretched out on my bed and began to enjoy her heels properly. I was almost oblivious to the outside world, I was nearly there, just me, Melissa and her fucking horny footwear. Downstairs, I think I heard the phone ring but I was just about ready to come. I couldn't tear my eyes off her shoes. I adored them, I adored the heels and her toes and just as I was about to go off like a pistol . . . I heard footsteps on the landing.

Christ, those were definitely footsteps and they were coming for my door. I couldn't be found like this with a porn mag, it'd be the worst thing in the world, so I grabbed the nearest thing to hand to cover up Melissa. There was a quick knock and the door opened and just in time I opened *Smash Hits* at a page I was reading that morning and there I was, with a vicious hard-on in one hand and a picture of Paul Weller in the other. My mother stood in the doorway, her eyes out on stalks. She swallowed once, and said, 'I think this obsession might be going too far. I'll tell Rik you'll ring him back later.'

She couldn't get out of there quickly enough.

Neither of us ever mentioned the incident again – we didn't need or want to. I do know that Mum must have said something to Dad, though I don't know exactly what, because when I came home from school next day he'd very kindly fitted a bolt to my bedroom door.

Rik told me at school that he'd been ringing to tell

me that he'd got a girlfriend. Her name was Louise Harrison and she sat next to him in biology. I was kind of miffed, because I quite fancied her myself and I used to love seeing her in her little blue sports skirt when we occasionally teamed up together to play badminton in PE. Rik was over the moon at having a girlfriend and all he talked about was Louise this and Louise that and Louise said this and me and Louise are going to go and see such and such film. I was chuffed for him and all that, but Jesus, after a while it became too much to take. I'm not sure if it was me just being jealous or whether I was simply bored with it but in the end I thought I'd have to say something. But I didn't. I couldn't, he was happy and what sort of a rotten mate would I be if I said something. Anyway, Rik had Louise and I'd got Paul.

By the time the next single came out, Rik and Louise were firmly established as long term boyfriend and girlfriend and I'd completely got used to the idea of sharing Rik with someone else and I wished them all the best together. Even if she was a dumpy little tart with no taste in music. I mean, Spandau Ballet, what was all *that* about?

* * *

My favourite album by The Jam was, and still is, *Sound Affects*. It was released at the back end of 1980 and had more than kept me going until 'Absolute Beginners'. That year also saw 'Funeral Pyre' come out as a single. It was released on 29 May, and went to number four in the charts. 'Funeral Pyre' sees Rick Buckler drumming away at the top of his game. He keeps his foot firmly on the accelerator all the way through, and delivers a performance that's as near to drumming nirvana as anything I've ever heard. Powerful, driving, thrusting – Rick's tempered venom on the kit is as angry as anything Paul's ever written.

Sound Affects has some works of genius on it. It's pure quality, a really special sound with a slightly psychedelic, arty feel to it. The album opens with 'Pretty Green'. This instantly catchy strike at naked capitalism features a bass line beating like a heart pumping money through the veins of those who have and ignoring those who have not.

Paul writes about power and the way in which it is measured, he says that that's done by either the pound or the fist. It's clear that this is a juicy slice of Marxist thinking aimed fairly and squarely at the new Thatcher parliament. Paul could see quite easily the way things in the country were going: rampant consumerism, second homes and not a thought from those in control for the people who needed them most. I loved this track, but I remember that Rik wasn't so keen.

My next fave track is the second song in. It's called 'Monday', and is too raw and personal a song to be completely made up. It *has* to be about Paul and his girlfriend, it's sung in a daydreamy kind of a way, like someone left alone with their thoughts, musing about their relationship. It's slow and thoughtful and doesn't stomp away like so many Jam tracks; rather it saunters after tea, going for a walk and looking at neighbours' front gardens like Mum and Dad used to. I loved it, but was envious that Paul and Rik had girlfriends and could share these feelings of examining their relationships with each other. Not that Rik had much time for that, he was going to see that clown Tony Hadley and his bunch of wankers in Spandau Ballet with Louise next weekend. Rik actually had the audacity to ask me if I wanted to go along with them. I'd have rather sawn both of my legs off with a rusty grapefruit knife but I didn't say as much – I told him I was going to Nottingham with the family.

I love 'Set The House Ablaze' and when I hear it

today, it's one hell of a signpost to what was happening within The Jam. The house is Paul's group, and he feels he's torched the thing – that's it, in a nutshell. PW sings about losing sight of his ambition, but the older I become the more it's dawned on me that, even though he clearly saw the end of the band in this track, he was also writing about antifascism, about George Orwell's essay, 'The Lion And The Unicorn' and (although not as much) about his novel, *Nineteen Eighty-Four*. Again, it's such a passion-fuelled number so typical of the band's heartfelt honesty it almost feels like it's a warning from Paul to steer clear of antipathy and to move forward, whatever the cost, without becoming bogged down in the mire of self-examination. Quite hippy-ish for one so mod.

'Man In The Cornershop' is the standout track for me on *Sound Affects*. It paints a vivid image of the differences between those earning a crust by their own hard work and staying small, like the man who runs the corner shop, and the grander experiences of the boss of the local factory. The song tells the tale of the two men and how they secretly envy each other, one wishing he was free to put up the closed sign whenever he wants, and the other jealous of his customer, owning such a large factory. To finish, Paul sticks the two characters in church on a Sunday and points out that in God's eyes, we're all equal whether we're bankers or bakers or whatever. Again, it's another song for Rik despite not really thinking so at the time. His dad was a banker, mine once a barber. They both made cuts where they had to, I suppose.

'Boy About Town'. Now, here's a classic Jam song.

Whenever I hear this, I feel that it's not so much about me at school, me in front of my peers, it's more about the way that maybe my family saw me. Swaggering, confident in my modernism . . . I felt removed from them, distanced. Some days, I even felt like I was dreaming them. This played in my head every time I left the house, even if I was just nipping out for a pint of milk. I'd begun to do my best to make sure that wherever I was, whenever I was out, I looked as sharp as possible. It wasn't just a mod thing; oh no – this went much further than that . . . this was a *Weller* thing.

The other tracks on *Sound Affects* are all excellent, but those are my top tracks. I haven't included 'That's Entertainment' in this selection because it has a different story to tell and deserves a piece all to itself.

'That's Entertainment' is possibly the song that non-Jam fans most associate with the band. It was recorded in September 1980 at the Townhouse Studios, Shepherd's Bush, and produced by Vic Coppersmith-Heaven along with The Jam. This song, for me, painted a picture of the life I was living. It painted the view from my window, my walk to school, the conversations I had while I was there and it painted my walk home and what I came home to. It was my world, and it was written in song.

It was the theme tune from the minute I got out of my bed to the moment I climbed back into it. 'That's Entertainment', with its wailing baby and blinking lamplight, the howling of a stray dog, the pneumatic drill constantly on overdrive, hard at work on next door's drive, the tomcat's cry that kept us awake every night, watching the news, watching the telly, the hot summer days – these were the things which drove me, and yet at the same time drove me to boredom. They combined, via this song, to chart my everyday living.

It's such a visual number, filmic even. The pictures it conjures up are harnessed for the single sleeve itself. Paul uncovered a BBC sound effects album in the studio whilst recording and was inspired to recreate the images on the album with tiny pictures of elements referred to in the song. It was never officially released as a single in the UK, only in Germany, but the band were so almighty over here that on import alone it crashed into the charts and peaked at twenty-one, which is a huge feat for an import with no publicity, and it stayed in the top seventy-five for seven weeks. I love it as much today as the first time I heard it.

It's a little known fact that the basis for 'That's Entertainment' was a poem of the same name which was submitted to Paul's publishing company by a very clever, unknown writer by the name of Paul Drew. I was submitting poetry of my own at the time, and wonder to this day if I was ever close enough to get as lucky as this guy. What an achievement.

Finally, after months of dithering and hanging around outside drama club, I summoned up the courage to go in and get on with it. It wasn't difficult – in fact it was the first time I learned that there's nothing more scary than fear itself. I felt instantly at home there. I was surrounded by pupils who all shared a love of the written word, of timing, of comedy and of a love of playing at being other people. We used to act out sketches from TV comedy shows. It was, I learned, just a tiny after-school club which had no plans to perform outside of its own little circle and we were content just to keep it that way: we could show off to each other without being seen to be show-offs by anyone else. Quickly, I gained confidence and drew on the fact that performance had been a big part of Grampa Lines's early life. Again, I felt acutely aware of the passing of more than a year since his death and I began to see how quickly time passed. I began to feel the need to develop my newly realised passion. I didn't have to wait for very long.

7

Precious

The first time I heard 'Precious' I thought that there'd been a horrendous mistake at the pressing plant. I almost phoned Polydor to check, because it didn't sound like anything that The Jam had done before. 'A Town Called Malice' was different enough, but for me at the time 'Precious' was such a radical change of sound, it was asking a lot from me. Until I'd heard it for the second time, that is.

The single sounded like disco but with added desperation. It's got a funky, relentless backbeat which thumps along like it's beating out panels and it's got Paul laying down a jangly guitar which kind of dances around on top of Bruce's heavy, pounding bass. Its jazz-funk and Paul's knocked-back vocal gives 'Precious' a sort of ghostly, echoey sense. It goes up and down, fades in and out and it's a hundred miles removed from what the rank and file fans at school had got used to. I was the only one who really, really liked it. I liked it because it sounded so good, so new, but I also liked it because I could hear Paul pushing himself, going to new places just like I wanted to. And was about to . . .

I'd made some great new friends, pupils who were in other forms and whose orbit I'd never have entered were it not for drama classes. One of my new friends was Lizzie Marlow, who looked like a younger version of Julie Walters, auburn hair in ringlets and a smile as wide as you like.

She was quite tiny, wore Kickers and was bold enough to cross cultural style boundaries hitherto uncharted by doubling them up with a boating blazer – some days she looked like a walking, talking dressing-up box. She dressed like Victoria Wood would, if you know what I mean. She was also quite a big Jam fan, had spectacular breasts and a boyfriend who was roughly the same size as our garage. Despite the spectre of her boyfriend James, we'd become quite close mates and we started our own little comedy writing club. Lizzie told me that James wasn't too keen at all on our weekly get-togethers round at her house – and she also told me that she rather liked the fact that he was not too impressed.

We would meet at Lizzie's house, which was almost identical to ours, or in The Link – the sixth-form block which everyone could use – after school where we'd churn out all sorts of nonsense, page after page of it. Reading it back we sat there like six-year-olds and just *howled.* Lizzie had eyes like an owl's and when they looked at you, they didn't so much look at you as entered you. So much so that I had to start concealing my thoughts when we were together, discreetly blotting them out, gently nudging them out of view with my foot when she wasn't looking, because I was entirely convinced that she could actually read my mind. After just a couple of weeks she'd started finishing my sentences for me . . . which was no bad thing because Lizzie's lines were far funnier than mine could ever be. There was an unwritten rule which existed between us, and that was that some things were best left unsaid. And we knew that it was the writing which bound us together like glue.

We'd sit across the desk from each other, frantically jotting down jokes and scribbling out scenes which didn't come up to scratch. 'That's a funny line. Write it down, David, before we forget it.'

'Um . . . sorry?'

'Are you staring at my cleavage?'

'No. Most certainly not.'

'Good. And make sure you don't. Now come on and get your biro out.'

Drama classes were great for another reason. I got to go and see real plays! Life was suddenly good for me. It had become rich and varied and I'd got a new haircut to match. It was basically a pair of curtains just like Paul's and was pretty high maintenance at the best of times. The curtains hung down over the front of my forehead and there was a kind of sticky-up bit at the back of my crown. If I didn't concentrate hard enough whilst styling this cut I ended up looking like a very passable impersonation of Helen Shapiro. In Garforth, this was a look best avoided; if I got it just a little bit wrong I may as well have waltzed down Main Street in a miniskirt.

One drama trip took me to Sheffield. We were going with the new Head of Drama, Marshall Sapherson, to see a play at the Merlin Theatre called *One In Ten* which was about disabled teenagers and how they coped with puberty and the added disadvantage of being in a wheelchair. Marshall had baggied the minibus for the night and it was due to leave the school gates at five fifty-five.

'Are you going out looking like that?'

I was about to leave for the theatre and Mum was staring at my new haircut. 'Yep. Why? What's wrong with my hair?'

'Nothing . . . it's just that . . . nothing. Your hair's fine . . .'

'It's just that *what*?'

'Nothing. It's just that . . . and please don't take this the wrong way, but you look like a girl.'

'Thanks for that.'

'Don't mention it. Do you want a pack-up?'

I was at the back of the bus and there was a spare seat next to me. Lizzie wasn't going because she was seeing James, but had made me promise to take extensive notes and to deliver a full critique when we met the next week. Marshall was just about to close the doors when from nowhere there was a blur of bright yellow plastic and a girl exploded into the seat next to me. I could hardly catch my breath – she was heart-stoppingly beautiful and a few years older than me. I'd never seen her at school before, she must have been in the sixth form and surely she needed a licence for those eyelashes. She looked at me, batted them once and the downdraft wrecked my hair for the rest of the night. She had big, brown cow eyes and hair the colour of an aubergine and smelled faintly of Silk Cut. I'd been taught to stand up when a lady sat down, but I couldn't because my knob was standing up like a cocked pistol. I took out my notepad to cover my crotch and started scribbling a poem – this girl beside me had inspired me! Maybe I'd send it to Paul.

The drive from Garforth to Sheffield took about an hour, maybe a little more, although it felt like approximately nine and a half billion years because that's what it feels like when you're trying desperately hard not to look at the person sitting next to you when that's all that you want to do.

The play was too shocking by far. Disability's a rum bedfellow, but this production was unbelievably excruciating at the best of times – and there weren't any of those throughout the entire, terrible ninety minutes. I watched most of the production through the cracks in my fingers – the rest of the time I was watching the beautiful girl wrapped up in yellow plastic.

As the curtain came down and the UB40 track, 'One In Ten' came up I mustered up the courage to say something to her. I turned and looked at her and she looked at me and suddenly my tongue hadn't got room to move inside my mouth because my heart took up most of the space. Despite that, I tried to sound articulate. 'I think, on the whole, that the sentiment's right. It's the execution which lets it down, though. The final scene with the epileptic fit was agricultural to say the least and we're not left with a sense of anyone caring about each other. It was all rather embarrassing, wouldn't you say? By the way, I'm David, David Lines. Pleased to meet you . . .' And I held out my hand to shake hers. This didn't sound like me. It sounded like me trying to sound like the way I thought older people talked to each other. I wasn't ready for this – shut up, you idiot.

She looked at me blankly and ignored my quivering hand. 'I thought it was beautiful.' And then she got up and quietly walked away.

On the return journey she sat up front in the passenger seat next to Sapherson and I spent the next hour drinking in the back of her head. It was the loveliest back of a head I'd ever seen. I could have stared at it till daybreak. When we pulled up into the car park she got out and said a cheery goodnight to Marshall who said goodnight back to her. I heard him say her name. It was the most beautiful name, it was Katherine.

The next morning I called for Rik on the way to school. His parents had just taken delivery of their brand new Mini Metro which was parked in front of their double garage. Inside, Selina Scott was on the box, sitting next to Frank Bough who was wearing a stripy jumper which made the telly go all wonky like what was left of his hair. He could have done with some conditioner on that lot. Frank looked like he'd had a hard night. 'How was your night at the theatre?'

'OK, thanks. What did you do?'

'I was working on my new Jam shoes. But I can't show you them yet – they're a surprise.'

'New Jam shoes? Really? What are they like?'

'I can't say any more. Let's just say . . . they're a bit special.'

This was the first I'd heard of new special secret Jam shoes. Honestly, Rik gave me the right hump sometimes. 'Do you want to come round tonight and make a new tape? I've got a new stereo coming today and guess what?'

I had a quick think but couldn't come up with anything. 'What?'

Rik's face lit up. 'It's only got tape-to-tape!'

'Skill! That means we can make two tapes, one each, in double-quick time.'

'I know. It's also got Dolby, a tape counter and all sorts of cool stuff we can play around with.'

Me? Jealous? Surely not. 'What about CD?'

'What about what?'

'CD. Don't tell me it hasn't got CD?'

'What's CD, Dave?'

Imaginary trumpets played a fanfare in my head. 'Oh, do try and keep up, Richard . . .'

I was eager to get to school and try and find out more about Katherine. On the way, I stopped and posted my poem about her to Paul. I didn't need to read it again to check for spelling mistakes or any other howlers because it was in my brain and I knew it off by heart and it was perfect, just like her. 'What's that you're posting?'

'This? Nothing, mate . . .' And oh, so much did I hate myself for feeling so petty. Why couldn't I just be honest with my best friend? It was only a poem, after all. Why should I have been so embarrassed about my feelings with my friend? Surely I wasn't that insecure.

There was something about the theatre, something which bit me that night. Despite the play turning out to be such a disaster, I felt the anticipation of the curtain coming up, I felt the electricity crackling behind it, I drank in the atmosphere coming from the stage and I knew then that this was for me.

The next morning I could feel it, deep inside me like a fresh spirit. It moved within me . . . and it was a blessing, cancelling out my envy over something as silly as a stereo and replacing those feelings with a sense that somehow I'd found something. The day just washed over me like a warm breeze and I didn't know if it was the theatre, or Katherine or maybe a bit of both. I didn't really care what it was that made me feel that way, I was just enjoying being happy.

After tea I biked round to Rik's. The Mini Metro gleamed in the driveway and I parked my BSA ten-speed next to it and rang the bell. Rik lived in a bungalow, and it was absolutely massive. There were so many corridors it must have been like living in a hospital. In fact, it was so gigantic I'd only just got used to where all the rooms were and which ones were which. It was easier finding my way round school for the first week. When I first needed to use the loo at Rik's place I actually got lost on my way to, and from, one of their many bogs. I still don't know how many there were and I'm not sure that they do either. The next time I had wanted to go, I'd prepared myself for not looking like a total idiot again.

I took off all of my Jam button badges and left a trail of them for me to follow all the way back from the loo to the lounge. It made me laugh both at, and to myself. 'What are you laughing at?'

'Nothing, Mrs Bowerman. Just me . . .'

I'd taken round that week's *Smash Hits* to show Rik the Jam poster that was inside. It'd also got the lyrics to 'A Town Called Malice' on it. Paul had started to wear sweatshirts and t-shirts made by Lonsdale and he was going for a boxing-coach look which, at the time, was dead cool. I'd already bought a whistle which I wore around my neck on a piece of string. The other thing that I'd noticed, was that he'd started wearing a button badge with a picture of Dennis the Menace on it. It became a top priority that I secured one as well.

I didn't know exactly what the hidden meaning behind the Dennis the Menace badge was but, knowing Paul, it was bound to be something overwhelmingly profound, full to brimming with hidden depths and all sorts of ironic comments about social injustice, class inequality and nuclear disarmament. Or maybe his girl-friend just gave it to him.

Rik opened the front door and we went inside to the kitchen – I'm pretty certain there was only one of them – and his mum made me a cup of coffee. 'Did your music centre arrive?'

'Yeah, it's so skill. I'll show you in a bit when Dad's finished setting it up for me. Won't be too long. Do you fancy a couple of frames of snooks whilst he finishes off with the wiring?'

'Yeah, all right.'

It was the end of February, and Rik was getting brilliant at snooker. I wouldn't have been surprised if he told me he was thinking of turning pro. He could perform all sorts of trickery like swerve shots and jumps and he could even stop the ball in its tracks and kind of reverse it back up the table. I don't know how he could calculate all those elaborate angles in his head in lightning-quick time like he did; I don't think I could have worked them out with a calculator. It was like playing snooker against someone half human and half protractor. After twenty minutes the score stood at a very impressive seventy-four points to eight. I couldn't believe it. I was seriously proud of my score as I'm normally worse than crap at snooker. I wanted to call a temporary halt to proceedings just so I could sit back and relish my points. I'd never potted a red and a black consecutively before and those two balls were responsible for my eight magnificent points.

I put down my cue and showed Rik my copy of *Smash Hits*. 'Look at the new poster that comes with it.'

Rik looked like he was weighing up an Old Master. He tilted it from side to side, studying it, holding it at arm's length, then brought it up to his face whilst all the time nodding approvingly and saying 'Mmmm' to himself. He held it up to the light and then passed it back to me. 'It's brilliant. I've got to get one for my room. I'll get a copy tomorrow.'

'Yeah, Paul looks dead cool. But listen, right, why do you think they've all started wearing this Lonsdale boxing gear? I mean, look at Rick Buckler, he's even wearing Lonsdale boxing boots.'

'I dunno, but I'm not keen on those boots. They're red, Linesy.'

'Yeah. Hey, I was wondering if maybe Paul had taken up boxing as a hobby.'

'Possibly, but then again he might just like the look.'

'It *is* a good look, isn't it?'

'It's a *very* good look. Very *original* . . .'

'Can you imagine Paul in a boxing ring having, you know, a real-life proper boxing match against someone? That would be just pure skill, right?'

Rik looked at me very seriously. Like I might have needed some sort of mental treatment. 'Um, I'm not sure that I can picture it. No, Dave. Anyway, who's his opponent?'

'I dunno . . . anyone. Let's have a think. How about Boy George?'

Rik slowly backed away whilst chalking the end of his snooker cue. He was giving it more attention than it deserved. Then again, that's probably why he was so excellent at it. 'You want me to imagine Boy George, in a boxing ring, with Paul Weller as his opponent?'

'Yeah. I can see it now. Boy George in his floaty white dress and his leggings underneath, with his make-up and that big, floppy hat and he's wearing this enormous pair of bright red boxing gloves. And he's sitting in his corner, right, and all his seconds would be attending to his make-up and doing his hair and checking his lippy. It'd be hilarious!'

'Right, Dave. Are you feeling OK?'

'Yeah, fine. Why?'

'No reason. So, what's Weller doing in the other corner whilst George's getting his eyebrows plucked?'

'Oh, he's just sitting there smoking a cigarette and having a drink.'

'What sort of drink do you think he likes?'

'God, Rik. I've never thought about that before. That *is* a good question. I think he probably likes a lager. Yes, he'd have a nice refreshing pint of lager before the fight started. And then the bell goes and Boy George starts prancing around the ring, waving his arms around like a big fairy and Paul's running around trying to catch him and then the theme tune to *Benny Hill* starts playing and it'd just be piss funny!'

Rik just stared at me, slowly shaking his spiky head. 'It's your shot, Linesy.'

'Oh, right.' I picked up my cue and took careful aim at the red ball closest to the near pocket. The red went in, followed by the black next to it and they were joined by my cue ball.

'Hard luck.'

I looked at Rik as he lined up his next shot and wondered quietly to myself if Paul played snooker.

At the back of my mind, though, were thoughts of Katherine. The way she moved, the smell of her hair . . . a new feeling bubbled up inside of me whenever I thought of her, and I could not keep that feeling pushed down any longer. I needed to tell someone about what happened to me the evening before and it seemed as good a time as any. I could tell Rik stuff like this, surely, he was my friend and I wanted to share it with him. Anyway, he was going out with Louise – he should be cool with talking about feelings and affairs of the heart and emotions. I thought I should give it a go. 'Look, I want to tell you about what happened last night.'

'Why, what did happen last night?'

'Everything happened. I sat next to a girl at the theatre and everything's been different since.'

'You sat next to a girl? That's brave of you.'

'Very amusing. Seriously, man, she was lovely. Just completely lovely.'

Rik sniffed and screwed his nose up at the same time. 'So, who is she? Whose form is she in?'

He drew back his cue, squinted down it and I replied, 'I've no idea whose form she's in – the thing is, I think she's in the sixth form.'

Rik's cue almost tore a hole in the baize when he heard this. That's four points to me, I thought. 'She's in the sixth? Then she must be maybe three years older than you. Forget about it – put her out of your head right now, because you've got about as much chance with her than you have of winning this frame.'

'Cheers, mate. Nice of you to say so.'

Rick scooted off to check on the progress in installing his stereo and came back a couple of minutes later with his portable cassette player. 'There's a hiccup with the speakers. This'll do for now.' He plugged it in and pressed play and 'Precious' filled the snooker room.

I heard this song with fresh, new ears. Listening then, after my revelation of the night before it sounded like a different tune entirely. The words had new meaning and as I sang along, it became as clear as can be that Paul was singing about me and the way that I felt about Katherine. Once again, he had got under my skin, understanding me more than I understood myself, feeling my feelings before I even knew about them. I was overcome and had to sit down for a minute.

'Fancy another frame, Dave?' Rik, of course, was oblivious.

'I'm OK, mate. I should be getting back. Actually, I'm not feeling too good . . .'

It was almost two weeks before I saw Katherine again. I was walking down the main corridor between lessons with Rik and a guy from my art class called Robin Parker. I couldn't stop looking at my new burgundy loafers which we got from Timpson's at the weekend. The leather looked cool against the white of my Tesco's terry towelling socks and in contrast with the silvery grey trousers I was wearing. I didn't think it got better than this.

'What are you looking at, Linesy?'

Rik blurts out, 'Don't interrupt him, Robin. He's staring at his shoes . . .'

I looked up and there she was. Katherine came towards me, maybe fifty feet away. My blood ran cold and I was instantly drenched in a hot sweat while my mouth felt like it was full of cotton wool. My heart was thumping out beats like Bruce's bass and in my head it was tapping out Morse. I looked away, looked back again and Katherine looked my way and smiled. Her eyes were even bigger and more beautiful than before. And, added bonus, she was only wearing a grey Lonsdale t-shirt!

'Hello.'

I was about to say hello back but didn't because someone had stapled my tongue to the roof of my mouth.

'Hi there,' replied Robin.

Wait a minute. This wasn't in the script. The smile hadn't been for me after all. I waited till she had passed down the corridor before pouncing on Robin. 'You know her?'

'Sure I know her. She's in my brother's form. That's Kath Blyton . . .'

And that was it, really. The rest of the day just faded away and when I went to bed that night I actually got down on my knees and prayed to Paul to help me find a way to get close to Katherine. This was what I wanted more than anything else in the world, so much so that every time I blinked I saw her face. I spent most of the next day staring into space and the most productive thing I did was to write the first verse of my ode to Katherine on the inside cover of my history book:

You're my very own personal drama queen,
And in my head we play out a scene,
Where we become lovers,
End up under the covers,
Lost in each other's charms.

Reading it now it doesn't just stink, it leaves a trail on its way to the toilet. But back then it meant a lot to me. Youth, eh?

The next day I met up with Rik outside the library. We needed to get some books out about trees and leaves to help us with our biology project. Rik had got hold of a thunderous tome on photosynthesis and we almost had to carry the thing between the two of us because it was so massive. It would have been perfect for pressing flowers as it weighed roughly the same as I did. We were walking up the steps from the library, past the office where matron famously dished out her horse pills when Rik stopped to bend down and tie the shoelace on one of his brogues. I'd never seen the top of his head from that angle before and it looked very much like there was a bald spot developing inside that fluffy nest of his, almost as if someone had taken a pair of nail scissors to the top of a busby and cut out a circle the size of a ten-pence piece. I decided it was best not to mention it to him, so I distracted myself by reading the notice board. I couldn't ignore the bald spot for too long, though. It was staring up from his head like a great, white eyeball and I swear it winked at me.

The desire to prod it with my finger became almost too much, but, luckily, it was then I spotted the poster up on the board. The drama department were planning on putting on a production of Sandy Wilson's *The Boy Friend* in three months' time, and were inviting pupils to audition. There was a list of characters from the play in one column and then an adjacent column where you wrote your name down against that of the part which you'd like. I turned back to Rik but as I did so, two words made me catch my breath. I looked back at the poster, and there, at the foot of the list written in red biro, was the name Katherine Blyton next to the part of Madame Dubonnet. Paul had answered my prayers, I just knew it. 'Rik, I want you to listen to me.'

'What about?'

'I want you to do something for me. I want you to stand here in front of this poster and look menacing for ten minutes. OK?'

'What are you talking about?'

'It doesn't matter, man. Just guard this thing with your life and don't you dare let anyone near it, understand?'

'No, Dave. I absolutely do not understand. What's going on?'

'It's just incredibly important, man. If anyone comes near this poster wave your hair at them. Keep them away at all costs and I'll be back as soon as I can.'

I ran down the corridor the wrong way, through the masses, sprinted into the library through the double swing doors and crashed into the Plays section and there, on the bottom shelf was a single copy of the script for *The Boy Friend*. My fingers scrambled through the pages, my eyes scanning every line till I found what I was looking for. Madame Dubonnet had a love interest and come hell or high water I was going to be it. I tore out of the library back to the notice board and there, next to the character of Percival Browne, I wrote my own name.

I got the part. Not out of any great dramatic

performance at the audition, but more due to nobody else wanting to play the part of a seventy-year-old man in a musical full of pretty young things. It didn't matter to me that I was the only one who went up for it – what mattered was that I got it.

The day I found out I skipped home on a cloud, my heart full of love and hope and achievement and just bursting with excitement. I did that all by myself, I told myself. I can't have been that bad or they would have got someone else in. I can't remember ever feeling so proud of myself; it was like someone had walked into a room, opened the windows and filled it with fresh, springtime air. 'Hi, Mum – I'm home!'

'You're full of the joys. What happened to you today?'

Mum was staring at some sort of computer manual. From the expression on her face you'd think she'd been asked to rewire the house. 'I've only got the best news in the world. I got the part in the musical! I'm going to play the part of Percival Browne and I get to be the boyfriend of Kath Blyton who's absolutely gorgeous and the world is so lovely and things couldn't get any better if they tried and if I don't shut up right now and stop talking about it then I'll probably start crying!'

My mother stared at me and said, 'You'll love it.

You were made to be someone else . . .' She gave me a hug. 'I'm so pleased for you. Well done, you big, clever boy.'

'Thanks. That's all I've ever wanted, you know.'

'What?'

'For you to be proud of me.'

Mum sniffed and wiped her eyes, 'Well, I am. Would you like me to help you learn your lines?'

'No, thanks. But there is something you might be able to help me with.'

'What's that?'

'Can you charleston?'

'Can I what?'

'Charleston. It's a dance, and Mr Hinkley said that I'm far from brilliant at it, which was nice of him because I'm actually rather crap at it. He said I should practise like mad. If I can't learn it then they won't let me in the show.'

'Oh right. I'm not sure. Go on, you show me and we'll learn it together.'

'No way. It's far too embarrassing. I'm going to my room now to have a crack at it – but I might show you later.'

Up in my room I put my twelve inch single version

of 'Town Called Malice' on the turntable. I was wearing my two-tone bowling shoes and my mauve and lavender boating blazer and the record started and opened with the Motowney bass bit which goes dum-dum-dum, der-der dum-dum-dum-der-dum and then there are these real close-up echoey finger clicks over Bruce's bass and I just *knew* that that's Paul clicking his fingers and then this lovely Hammond organ sweeps in and there I was, doing the charleston to 'Town Called Malice' in my bedroom. It turned out to be a great tune to charleston along to, it's absolutely perfect. You had to kind of place both your hands close to your chest, palms away from you, fingers pointing upwards, and then you made these jerky, circular motions first one way, then the next, whilst kicking your heels out, backwards, at the same time. I was really into it in just seconds! The tempo could not be better to charleston to and I was conscious of how absurd I must have looked and I was laughing whilst dancing, because honestly, I knew how much of a prize wanker I must have appeared but it just didn't matter to me because I was enjoying myself so much.

It occurred to me then how apt a musical it was for me. The only thing it left out was Lambrettas. There were boating blazers and penguin shoes stage left, right and centre.

When the song slowed down, I slowed my dance down, too and just skipped along to it when it dawned upon me that this was almost exactly the same style of dance that the skins and the rude boys in their braces and their Doc Martens and their pork pie hats did when they got up at Youthy and danced around in a circle to The Specials and The Beat and The Selector and Bad Manners. How could anyone like Bad Manners with that fat idiot with the tongue? He was disgusting, nothing more than a pantomime dame in Doc's. Tears of laughter ran down my face and like a fool, I was doubled over in hysterics at what a tit end I must have seemed but I kept dancing because I just didn't care.

I'd never be able to keep a straight face when I next saw them on the dance floor. I may well have looked like a complete fairy doing that dance, but I was truly connected with the music and then I began to bob my head out in time to the bass, just like Bruce did when he was playing. The crescendo came, and in the bit where I'd normally leap up in the air like Paul would with a scissor-kick, instead, I instinctively performed a sort of charleston leap and where before I'd pretend to play guitar I just did this big, circular, hand-motion thing. I'd cracked it!

I'd learned to charleston and had also made it mine, individual, special to me. Thanks to Paul Weller, my part in the production was secure. I read the script more than thirty times and, along with keeping up with my private poetry, I had developed a sneaking suspicion of where I wanted to go in this world.

I was as certain as I could be at almost fifteen what I wanted to do with my life – and the fact of the matter is, I wanted to be a writer. I'd read *The Boy Friend* till I was blue in the face, and it was good, but I began to believe that I could have done better. I could see where it works and where it doesn't work, where it lifts itself up and which parts flag and drag it down and I'd have cut a couple of numbers which, frankly, got in the way of the momentum of the story. I decided to write a play of my own, just to prove to myself that I could do it. I wasn't sure what it was going to be about, so went downstairs for some inspiration and a Findus French Bread Pizza. The topping scalded the roof of my mouth and skin hung down inside like wet socks off a radiator.

What I was really aware of while I was rehearsing,

and it's something I often think about even now, was whether theatre was in my blood. Did I dig it so much because of Grampa Lines's thwarted ambition? He had been a song and dance man until his friend and partner died in an accident. Maybe I was reliving his lost dream? It was obvious that this love of theatre had skipped a generation; Dad didn't seem to understand. While Mum helped me with my lines, Dad talked about my crazy ideas and writers and actors all being 'a bit dodgy'and at my age I should have been thinking about a trade instead of poncing around like a big fairy. Mum told him it was just a stage I was going through and Dad said that if I didn't snap out of it soon he'd gladly help put me through it . . .

One week until opening night. I was nervous, we all were. But there was a growing sense of confidence, too; both cast and crew were nearly there, it was within our grasp. As a team, we weren't bad at all. My singing voice was benefiting from David Hinkley's extracurricular attentions. 'When you open your mouth, I want to hear it, listen to it come from deep within you.'

'Yes, sir.'

'Good boy.'

Lizzie was also in our play. She had the part of Dulcie, a pupil at Madame Dubonnet's finishing school. Lizzie had such great presence; she was so full of electricity on stage. She and Kath worked really well together and became friends. As an ensemble we were all good, but it was Kath who really stood out. She was so serious about her part. Kath had been treading the boards for more than four years and was so much more experienced than the rest of us. Having her on board was almost like having a Hollywood star walk amongst us. Kath was resolute in the knowledge that she would be an actor. Her unshakeable belief and steadfast trust in herself, her ambition and ability were nothing short of intoxicating. Just being in the same room as her was enough to inspire me tenfold. If Kath could be an actor – as I truly believed she would be – then maybe I could make my living as a writer. In our school, if you aspired to anything more than a miner or a milkman then people looked at you like you were insane. This is the thing that I learned from Kath above all: to have the courage of my convictions and to find the strength of my nature. That and how to hit my mark.

The character I played, Percival Browne, was Madame Dubonnet's long-lost love, and our rekindled relationship formed the backstory to the musical's central theme. We had a duet together and we had to meet up often, outside regular school hours, outside normal rehearsal time, to get it spot on. Kath was a consummate professional even then, and when she started to sing it sounded as if somehow there was a lark lodged deep within her larynx. I, however, sounded more like a tit.

'I'm sorry, Kath. Can we try that again, please?'

'That's all right, David. Just take your time and try to relax, yeah?'

Relax? How on earth could I possibly relax? That just wasn't going to happen when I was about to sing a song to Katherine Blyton about how much I loved her in the past and how could I possibly forget the love that we knew and now that we've found each other all these years later all the emotions keep on flooding back and . . . and . . . just calm down, man. Take. Deep. Breaths. I asked myself, what would Paul do in a situation like this? What would Paul do? I'll tell you what Paul would do, he'd just get on with it and sing to her. That's it! I'd got it! I'd sing the duet with Kath just the same way that Paul would sing it, I'd sing my bits and sound like Paul would. That was it, that'd help me get through it. I took a glug of water and launched into it.

I was halfway through my verse when Kath waved at me. I waved back at her and then she waved like she was trying to flag down a police car in a terrible emergency. Oh, hold on – it dawned on me that maybe she wanted me to stop. 'David, I hope you don't mind me mentioning it, but why on earth are you doing an impersonation of Tommy Steele?'

'Sorry?'

'Where did all these estuary vowels come from all of a sudden? This isn't "Half A Sixpence", darling . . .'

Oh my God – she called me darling! 'Tommy Steele? Christ, I'm sorry, Kath – I don't know what happened there. I'm just a bit nervous, that's all.'

She batted her eyelashes and said, 'Just be yourself, honey, and it'll all come together. Just be yourself . . .'

Me? Be myself? That was pretty difficult when I spent so much time trying to be anything but me. 'Thanks, Kath. Thanks for the advice. Shall we try it again from the top?'

'I don't think so. Let's wrap it up here. I've had more than enough for one day.'

Oh, all right. I was just getting into it. 'Can I walk

home with you, please then?' Why had my voice suddenly gone all high?

Kath laughed a little bit and said, 'You can if you like.' Then she slung her Chelsea Girl bag over her shoulder, flicked her hair back and turned to me. The late autumn light crept in through the music-room window and she smiled and said, 'It's a lovely evening for it.' It most certainly was.

We walked through the sunny, empty streets of the Grange estate, which was where Katherine lived. Our house was on the Wimpey estate, and it had been the show home for when our estate was built, about twenty years ago.

The houses on the Grange estate were bigger, more like the houses on Rik's street. The front lawns were longer, wider and some of them even had three cars parked in the drive. Lots of houses on our street were pebble-dashed but there weren't any of those to be found around Kath's estate; instead the pebbles were on the drives, not stuck to the front of the houses. Faded laburnum dripped down onto the pavement, neat lawns were marked out with crisp edges. It's lovely, I thought to myself – this is exactly the sort of place where Katherine should live. She looked like she lived there, she was comfortable there and she was such a star that I half expected to look down at the pavement and see her handprint in a flagstone with her name signed underneath it. This was Garforth's Walk of Fame. I wondered how she'd feel if I asked her to autograph my copy of the play?

We had made small talk to begin with, but we were soon talking about serious stuff, things that I had wanted to discuss with Rik but had bottled out at the last minute.

'Did you always know that you wanted to be an actor?'

'David, I knew from the moment that I could first think for myself. There was nothing else in my life and there never will be. Once I lifted the lid on that dressing-up box there was no turning back, not for one moment. It was a calling, and I know this sounds all arty and pretentious, but it was just that – an almighty calling.'

There was an edge to her voice. An urgency that came with conviction, like she'd been bursting to tell someone – anyone – this. She spoke with such intensity I was slightly shaken by it, and then I wondered if she'd been rehearsing her answer, practising for when she's famous and giving interviews in Cannes.

'Your mum and dad must be very proud of you.'

She blew her fringe out of her face with an upwardly directed exhalation of Silk Cut and sighed a big sigh. 'They are, but I do feel a bit fucking guilty some of the time. Well, most of the time.' She took a can of Lilt out of her bag, lifted the ring pull, swigged and passed it over. This act of intimacy wasn't lost on me and I savoured the moment much more than I did the drink.

'Thanks. Why d'you feel guilty? What have you got to feel guilty about?'

'Oh, David, it's just positively awful. Well, the thing is, my mum's a nurse, my big sister's a nurse and my little sister's probably going to be a nurse as well. They're all doing really, you know . . .'

She looked at me as if I should know what she meant, and she raised her eyebrows and nodded at me, but I just shook my head back at her. I was suddenly struck by the thought that this is the first grown-up conversation I'd probably had with anyone. I'd never had a conversation like this before. Kath seemed so . . . well, she was a proper woman. I bet she's even got a cheque book, I thought. 'Go on,' I said. I had an idea where her house was and it wasn't far from where we were, just around the next bend. I didn't want our time together to end so I deliberately started walking slowly to draw it out, nonchalantly strolling along with my hands in my pockets and staring up at the sky, considering the clouds.

Kath continued. 'Well, they're all doing incredibly selfless jobs. They're all being ungrudgingly benevolent and they do so much for so many poorly people every single day of the week and the money's not exactly brilliant, you know?'

'Isn't it? I didn't know that.'

'No, it's rubbish, and they're bringing such a lot of good into the world and they work so hard, and never once do they complain when they come home, not even after a terrible day, and what they do is just, you know, so worthy and so vital.'

I could see her point, but there was another side to it. 'But don't you think that what you'll do for a living, the way you'll lift people out of their lives and carry them off and away from their problems, their drudgery, will be just as vital? To entertain people, to make them laugh, to bring some light into their lives

– I'd say that was pretty fucking worthy and vital, Kath.'

We were outside her house and she looked at me with a big, beaming smile. I had said the right thing. Her arms were crossed and her head was tilted on one side and the curve of her left breast under that Lonsdale t-shirt started to draw my gaze just a little bit too much. 'That's beautiful. That's a fucking lovely thing to say.'

I didn't know *what* to say then, so I decided not to screw it up by opening my mouth so instead I just smiled back and kind of shrugged my shoulders like some kind of an idiot. Better to let her think I was a moron than open my mouth and prove her right.

'Why don't you come in for a cup of tea?'

Right then there was nothing in this world I wanted more.

I sat in Kath Blyton's kitchen with a pot of tea on the table between us. She sat opposite me. Milk in a jug, sugar in a matching bowl and a plate of digestives completed the scene. It was like a dream. I shouldn't have been there, but I was.

'Shall I be mother?'

There's a thought.

'What about you?'

'No, I'm fine. You carry on – you be mother.'

'I meant what about you, David. Have you any idea what you want to do with your life?'

'Oh, I'm very clear now. I've just made up my mind what I want to do with it.'

'What? Tell me – no, let me guess! I think you might very well want to . . . be in a pop group!'

'Why on earth would I want to be in a pop group?'

'Because it's the sort of thing you'd be brilliant at. You'll need to learn how to sing properly, mind, but you've certainly got the look.'

Kath poured the tea. There were freckles on her arms and, underneath the wide, pine table, our toes were touching. I didn't move my foot away; it liked it down there. 'So tell me, David Lines, what *are* you going to do with your life?'

'Me? Oh, I'm just going to be a writer.'

Kath's eyes widened, and then it hit me who she reminded me of – Kath Blyton was the living spit of Liza Minnelli. It was the eyes. The eyes and the hair. Strike me down now as I live and breathe, she was Judy Garland's tortured daughter and she's just poured me a cup of Typhoo. She was a superstar in our school and this felt like spending time with an Oscar winner. 'Well, good for you! Fucking hell – a writer! God, how romantic. What sort of things will you write?'

In my head I heard myself speaking, but these words stayed firmly locked inside my mouth. One day I'll write a book, and you'll be in it and it will be about how you, you and Paul Weller, inspired me to become a writer. 'Um . . . spy novels. And maybe some thrillers,' I said.

Kath raised her mug at me across the polished table and we clinked cups, like at a wedding. She looked me in the eye, stood up, held her tea aloft and said, 'To the arts – for there is no higher calling!'

I got up as well, raised my brew and repeated, 'To the arts!' It felt like we'd made a pact with each other there, a special deal. I thought about trying to give her a hug, because, let's face it, that's what arty people do, when the kitchen door opened and in walked a man who was clearly Kath's father. He moved just like her, sort of gliding inside, like a secret note being pushed under a door at midnight.

'Hello, Kate. Good day? Who's this, then?' He had a Geordie accent and a big, happy smile.

'Dad, this is David Lines and we're both in the play

together. David, I'm happy to say, is my seventy-year-old love interest . . . David – this is my dad.'

We shook hands. I instantly liked this man.

'Dad, David here's going to be a writer.'

'Are you now?'

'Well, I'm going to give it a go, Mr Blyton.'

'Then make sure that you do. Good luck, then. Pleased to meet you . . .'

And then I ran home. I literally ran all of the way home. I ran through the front door and into the hall and up the stairs. I ran into my room and I put *All Mod Cons* on and I listened to Paul sing 'Fly'. 'Fly' is the most exquisite love song. It's tender and harsh and modern and touching. It's as personal as a prayer and there's an intimacy that comes through from hearing Paul's fingertips squeak as he moves them up and down the frets if you listen closely enough. 'Fly' was recorded on 16 August, 1978, at RAK Studios, deep in the leafy heart of St John's Wood in London. It swings between gentle, touching parts and then raises its game to become more brutal in the bridge as well as the chorus and this, quite clearly, heralded their new-found sound.

At that moment, 'Fly' was everything to me. It was the theme tune to which, in my mind, Kate and I danced till daybreak. Her dad called her Kate, and now I would, too.

After 'Fly', I listened to 'English Rose'. I sat on the edge of my bed and thought about her. Paul not only described this girl in the song, he described the way that I felt about Kate. We had made a deal that day, a pledge to be true to ourselves and I knew that we'd never break it. I replayed the last few hours, minute by minute in my head. I couldn't believe it – I didn't do anything wrong, I didn't make a proper prat of myself – not once. That afternoon had been a potential personal warzone for me, a minefield in the making, and somehow I managed to pick my way through it and avoid making any idiot comments.

There was a knock on my door and Mum stuck her head round. She looked surprised to see me doing nothing, just sitting there and not having a wank.

'What's up?'

'Nothing, just thinking about things.'

Mum came and sat down next to me, put her arm around my shoulder and gave me a squeeze.

'Anything I can help you with?'

I wanted to tell her about Kate, about the promise we made, about how lucky I felt when we accidentally touched toes under the table. I wanted to tell her about the ember from Kate's cigarette and how, as she sucked slowly on it, the orange glow was reflected in her eyes. But I didn't tell her any of that. 'It's just nerves,' I said.

'You're bound to be nervous, it's opening night soon – Friday, right?'

'Yes. And you're all coming?'

'Of course we are. We're all very excited. I'm having my hair done in the afternoon, especially for the occasion.'

'Is Dad excited?'

Mum smiled and patted my knee. 'He's not really one for musicals . . .'

8

Music For The Last Couple

Again, recorded at the Townhouse Studios. This album track was the result of a studio jam session and contains only the one line of lyric. It's dead arty: there's a load of sound effects at the beginning, a bluebottle buzzing, the squirt of an aerosol can, some cowbells, tom-toms, then quiet followed by a jangly guitar riff. As Percival Browne, I had many more lines than just the one in this but its title always rings clear as meaning something special to me. In my mind, Kate and I were that last couple.

Before I knew it, it was Friday. Opening night.

Nerves had been gnawing away at my intestines all week, feasting on my fears and starving me of sleep. It didn't matter then, because I couldn't feel more awake, electricity fizzed through my veins and my eyes stung as I held back tears that bristled with excitement and nervous energy. Was that how Grampa Lines felt when he went on stage? Was that how Paul felt? Did nerves get to him, too?

They must have. The feeling filled my eyes, ears, nose and mouth – it felt like it might even drown me. In an attempt to hold onto the glorious feeling of the first time I went on stage in front of an audience, I wrote a detailed diary after the performance, describing what happened from moment to moment and I deliberately wrote it in the present tense as I thought it added to the dramatic effect. It's a mark of how deeply it affected me that I tried to get down almost every second. Here's what I wrote more than twenty years ago:

Time: 4.32 p.m. and we're all standing centre-stage having a big group hug. There's so many of us, it reminds me of country dancing back at junior school. Cast, crew, costume, musicians, make-up, lighting and scenery people standing in a semicircle with our arms around each other's shoulders and waists, waiting till curtain-up and propping each other up in the final few hours till kick-off. We're nearly there – can we get through this together? I'm not sure, but I do know that we're going to have a bloody good go!

4.45 p.m. I'm in Kate's dressing room. None of us have a dressing room, but Kate's decided to move into the pottery workshop which backs onto the stage and she's managed to make this her own. It's incredibly impressive, a real dressing room for a real star.

A huge great mirror in a golden frame stands on top of the potter's wheel and rests against the back wall. Golden Christmas fairy lights, lit up and draped around the frame sparkle and twinkle against dozens of good luck cards of all shapes and sizes. There are so many bouquets, it's like a florist's shop in here. The air is heady with the scent of lilies and a pair of pink teddy bears hold hands next to her make-up bag which is, in fact, a holdall. Kate's not here, so I leave the card which I've made for her, and prop it up against the bears. It's a piece of white, A4 cartridge paper folded in half with a black and white picture of Audrey Hepburn smoking a cigarette in a holder stuck to the front. I cut it out of the Radio Times *with a pair of Mum's pinking shears to give the edges a fancy finish. Inside, I've written 'Thanks for everything –*

good luck, and let's have fun! Love, David.' I stand back, peering at myself in Kate's mirror and the halo of gold thrown out from the fairy lights illuminates my face like a hundred thousand buttercups held up under my chin. It's dazzling, I take a mental snapshot and quietly walk away.

4.56 p.m. Neil Harding's throwing up into the fire bucket. That's a good place to spew up, in all that sand. Nerves? Could be. Smells more like Pernod. And judging by the vivid colour of the vomit it looks like he's been mixing it with black-currant. Idiot. Thank Christ he's only got a very minor role. What a prize wanker, he doesn't deserve to share the same stage as Kate and I'm considering dropping him in it to Sapherson. We can't afford to be let down by some joker like that pube-head.

5.10 p.m. Spend the next fifteen minutes gulping down two extra-large bottles of ice-cold dandelion and burdock. Thought it would be nice and soothing on my throat, but all it's done is freeze my vocal cords. They feel like someone's in there, squeezing them, and when I open my mouth to speak, all that comes out is a squeak. Nip outside for a fag to try and defrost them.

5.22 p.m. There's real tension backstage now. If the power should fail tonight we need not worry – you could run the lighting off the electricity in the air. Nothing in particular's happened, you can just taste it in the atmosphere.

5.58 p.m. Just over an hour to go and it's hotting up good and proper. The entire cast seem to be wandering around each in their own little world, reciting their lines under their breath like they're chanting a secret mantra. I'm doing it as well, and mid-flow am struck by the notion that I'm Percival Browne now. I'm Percival Browne for tonight and for the next six nights in a row and what I'm not going to be doing, is Being Paul Weller. It feels like I'm cheating on Paul, going with someone else behind his back. I put this stupid thought away in a cardboard box marked Idiot. I don't need this now – what I need, is to concentrate.

6.10 p.m. Richard 'Banger' Jameson's just sidled over and he's carrying with him an enormous pair of lurid pink tights and wearing a look of complete and utter desperation. I don't blame him, I'd look like that with those things under my arm.

'All right, Linesy?'

'All right, Banger. Not bad, you?'

'Yeah. Kind of. I want to make you an offer.'

'What sort of an offer? What are you on about?'

'It's quite straightforward – I want you to wear these tights for me.'

'You perv.'

'Look, I'm asking you nicely.'

'You are a mad person.'

'No I'm not, what I am, though, is feared by people in this school. They shit themselves when they see me coming and I like that, it works to my advantage. If I wear these tights on stage my reputation'll go downhill quicker than Buster Bloodvessel in a fucking shopping trolley.'

He's got a point, Banger will look like a prize dick. 'I see what you mean, old son. That's not the sort of fearsome image you want to be projecting.'

'Too right. Especially when I'm looking to expand my interests into the dinner ticket business. Very lucrative, I'll have you know, Linesy.'

'So what do you want me to do about it?'

'Easy. You give me your black tights for the fancy dress party scene and I give you my pink ones.'

'And?'

'And what?'

'And what's in it for me?'

'Nothing.'

'Nothing?'

'Not right now, but let's say you swap with me, lend me your nice, smooth, black tights, then one day, and that day may never come, but one day you may call on me for a favour and that favour will be granted. If you had a problem, then your problem would become my problem. If you had an enemy, then that man would become my enemy. And he would fear you. Capisce?'

'Bless you.'

'That's Italian for do you fucking understand?'

'Oh, right, yes – have my tights with pleasure. They're all yours.'

'Nice one. I won't forget this.'

I go and try my new tights on. I don't mind them, they're much more Percival's colour.

6.35 p.m. Tummy's doing crazy cartwheels. I wonder if Paul feels butterflies like I do. These are proper nerves, and I can't lose mine – I must stay cool. There's some last minute set painting going on and repairs are being made to the trellis in the garden scene where that clown Harding fell through it and Lizzie's lost her costume and everyone's smoking and it's just busy, busy, busy. I peep around the curtain to see if all the chairs have been put out yet and I'm astonished to find Mum, Dad, Chris and Phil seated smack in the front row. People are still putting chairs out behind them – how did they get in so early? Dad's pouring two cups of coffee out of the tartan thermos and Mum's busy unwrapping some sarnies from silver paper. Chris is lost in his Rubik's cube and Phil's reading a comic. They really don't look like they want to be here for one second. Dad looks like Grampa from up here, and he suddenly looks up and we catch each other's eye and I don't know why, but we just do, we both look away instantly and I dive back behind the curtain. To make it easier, I think I'll imagine that it's Grampa Lines out there instead of Dad. He liked the stage, so I'll do it for him.

6.48 p.m. Miss Rose appears. She's Marshall Sapherson's deputy and she's running late, she was supposed to have Brylcreemed my hair back half an hour ago. Out comes the red and white tub, out comes the comb and then a handmirror and there, staring back at me is the face of Grampa Lines. I know that the theatre is supposed to be full of superstition, but I've seen a ghost this evening. I don't mind, I'm not scared, I think this is a friendly one.

6.53 p.m. Still no sign of Kate. I'm almost in a blind panic – where is she? Half of me thinks she's given it up because I might make her look crap next to me. Not even I could make Kate look crap. I try her dressing room but it's deserted.

6.54 p.m. I'm beside myself. Drenched, dripping in cold sweat, I feel like I might pass out. I need oxygen, I'm a fish out of water and I crash through the fire doors out into the cool night air, drinking it in and feeling my heart thumping to get out.

I can't believe it. There she is. Kate is in full make-up, full costume; a scarlet, satin, full-length evening gown with a red feather boa draped gracefully over her shoulders. Kate's wearing red silk evening gloves up to her elbows and is smoking a cigarette in a holder with one hand and the other's cradling a glass of white wine. She's leaning against the wall, her hip out at an angle. Kate is stardom personified and I catch my breath as I catch sight of her. If I'm putting her on a pedestal then at least there's a chance that I might be able to see up her dress.

'Kate, you should come inside. It's just seconds to curtain-up.'

Smoke leaves her lips and fills an empty sky. 'Cool your heels, darling, I'm just getting into character. Now, be calm and just follow my lead . . .'

And with that she drops her cigarette, grinds the thing

under her heel, turns, and then she glides, she just glides *back inside, through the pottery studio, past my unopened card and out the other side, down the corridor, up the steps, into the wings and out onto the stage. Kate hits her mark with such precision and polished skill it's obvious to everyone that she's head and shoulders above the rest of us. I'm watching her now from the wings and there's a serenity to the scene, a hush, the audience can't bear to take their eyes off her. I'm surprised how calm I am now, my nerves have turned to nothing and I'm mouthing Kate's lines along with her. I know every word that's coming out of her mouth and my entrance is just seconds away. Someone pats me on the shoulder and wishes me 'Good luck', I take a deep breath and step out onto the stage and feel the heat from the lights hit my face.*

That's where my theatre diary ends, but that evening meant so much, it could have been yesterday.

The first thing that struck me was the audience. I couldn't see them, and I couldn't see Grampa Lines. Even though this was unexpected, I didn't mind at all; it was much more personal, private and intimate, like when it was just Kate and I rehearsing. It was just the two of us, alone on the big stage. She held my gaze as I delivered my lines and she nodded encouragingly and touched my arm with her gloved hand when it was her turn to speak. I wasn't expecting it, we didn't rehearse it, but it was a lovely gesture because it made me feel like we were on the same side and in it together. The audience had picked up on that; they were laughing more, they were beginning to relax.

I could hear the audience moving about – oh no, were they leaving? They weren't, they were just feeling comfortable enough to move around in their seats. I think I knew by then that we were on to something good. The scene was over and we got a nice exit round – which is when they clapped when we left. Kate had told me that she loves getting them and hoped we'd get one that night. It felt so special.

Backstage, and between hissed 'How do you think it's going?' and 'Nice one, Linesy', there was a very strong sense of us coming together to make something clever and real. Something that was a joy to be a part of. This was the first time, outside of my family, I'd ever felt so appreciated, or wanted, or even required. It was a feeling too strong ever to disappear and I loved it, I adored it because I felt that I belonged.

After the interval the audience enjoyed themselves even more, and we picked up on this straightaway and

I asked Kate who was really in charge there, us or them? As a cast we were enthused even further by the audience reaction and this drove us and drove us and I raised my game by trying to use much more of the stage, trying to match Kate by making big, dramatic gestures which we didn't rehearse. She didn't seem to mind and I caught her smiling and I thought I'd actually impressed her. Never mind that – I'd impressed myself for once. God, how I wanted that night to never, never end.

When the final party scene came it really did feel like we were having a party! Our voices lifted even higher, and we sang with big, open mouths and huge white smiles and the final number where we were all on stage together was a true delight to be a part of. We were in a line and I looked up it, then down it. Everyone was amazing and we would be again the next night and even though I couldn't wait to do it again – I could have done it again right there – I wanted to halt time right there, capture the magic of my first night and pour it into a little bottle so I could taste it again and again and again.

I saw Lizzie, Hazel Rimmer, Julia Jackson, Banger in black tights, Gary Street, Ann Robson, the lovely

Claire Jackson from the orchestra and then I looked sideways and there was Kate, whose hand I was holding. I was also holding hands with Gary Street, but it didn't mean anything. All of those friends, all of us having spent the best night together, it was almost too much for me and I quickly bit my bottom lip as I felt a tear spill over. I didn't know how she knew, but she did, and Kate took a bow and lifted her left arm up high – and as I bowed, her red glove softly wiped away my salty tear.

I could see the tear stain on her long glove. I looked out into the audience as the lights came up and there was the ghost of Grampa Lines sitting next to my mother. He nodded his head and smiled and as the curtain came down, I stepped back.

After the show, Mum, Dad, Chris and Phil were waiting for me at the bottom of the spiral staircase. Loads of other parents were milling around, drinking teas and coffees from plastic cups. They gave a ripple of applause and then we all had a hug. 'Well done, David. I'm very, very proud of you. You've got a lovely singing voice and that was a fine charleston, after all that worrying.'

'Thanks, Mum.'

'That was brilliant, son. I enjoyed that. You were great, you all were.'

'Dad, you hate musicals. How much of it did you sleep through?'

'None, I'm sorry to say – the chairs weren't comfy enough . . .'

Chris and Phil were giggling about something with each other. 'What are you two laughing about?'

'You were holding hands with that boy with the big bottom,' spluttered Phil from behind his hands.

'It was just for the play, Phil.'

'Is he your boyfriend?'

'No, he is not my boyfriend.'

Then Gary Street waddled past, ruffled my hair and pinched my arse. 'See you tomorrow, Linesy, you puff!'

Phil fell into Chris, almost toppling over at what Streety said. I turned down the offer of a lift home as I wanted to be on my own for a bit so I said that there was an after-show debrief and that I wouldn't be too long.

It had gone eleven, and I was walking slowly through the soft rain that fell on the good roofs of Garforth. I'd been walking for half an hour with Claire Jackson, the clarinet player from the school orchestra who'd famously been going out with Jon Baker since they met on their first day at primary school. Claire was a beautiful girl, her skin like vanilla ice cream and her blonde hair that swung down her back was as blonde as Anthea Redfern's, only natural. She had these lovely cheeks which plumped out, like she was hiding marshmallows in them. We didn't really know each other very well at all, so it was nice just to walk together without actually saying anything very much. It was very comforting and calming, just being with someone else and walking, silently, in the rain.

Neither of us, it was clear, wanted to be at home right then. And neither of us asked the other one why, so we just walked, and walked. I didn't mind the rain because the Brylcreem made it slide off my head and down the back of my neck. At least I'd still got cool hair in the middle of a rainstorm. Claire saw the rain that ran down the collar of my Harrington, linked arms with me and held her clarinet case over our heads as we walked on through the night. We hadn't spoken for twenty minutes. She was warm and I could smell her perfume and she had sweet, plastic cup coffee breath. The rain became heavier. We stopped and I broke the silence. 'Where do you live?'

'Here.'

Claire pointed at the house in front of us, and then she leaned forwards and placed the most delicate and tender of kisses on my cheek. 'Goodnight, David. And thanks for . . .'

'Goodnight, Claire Jackson.'

The rain slowly ceased as I walked the half mile home. Mum and Dad's bedroom light was still on and when I walked up the path and put my key in the door, it went out. Like a, well, light. I went to the kitchen and dried my hair with a tea towel then poured myself some milk into a German beer glass that Dad brought back from a business trip. I took one of his cigarettes from the packet on the side, opened the back door and sat on the step, drinking my milk and smoking. I blew smoke at the stars and wrote up the night in my diary. When I'd finished I went upstairs and got under the shower. Standing there under a torrent of hot water, running mascara, Brylcreem, shampoo, conditioner, it was a wonderfully cleansing feeling and I watched the night run down the plughole. I really did it that night. I got into bed, turned out the light, closed my eyes and before I knew it, I was fast, fast asleep.

It was the last night of the show and the week-long

run of *The Boy Friend* came to a close all too soon. I was sad. Those last seven days had been the most sparkling, special time for me. When I woke each morning there had been stars in my eyes, hope in my heart and being alive, feeling alive, had never felt like that before. I felt like I was treading the past as well as the boards, and in spirit I could feel that Grampa was with me, too, acting out his old dream alongside me. It'd been fun being an actor. One of the hundreds of best bits about it had been when kids stopped me in the corridor and asked for my autograph. I *loved* that! I even thought about having signed pictures printed. I wasn't letting it go to my head, though.

At breakfast earlier that week: 'David, why are you wearing a monocle?'

'I'm staying in character. It's called method acting.'

'But you're eating Sugar Puffs. Does Percival eat Sugar Puffs?'

'Of course he does, Mum. They're all the rage *sur la plage* . . .'

I'd enjoyed the French Riviera look, it was very mod indeed. I wished it was something that Paul would get into, it'd suit him. I thought about dropping him a line, pointing him in the right direction.

It was the closing-night party. Brylcreem is impossible to shift unless you're under a shower, so I was happy to wear it à la Percival Browne for the wrapping-up party. Kate was there, without her better half, and even though we could both see what was going to happen I still went through with it. It's like we were acting out another scene together. Kate knew what I was going to say, I knew what she was going to say, but still, I just had to ask. 'Hi, Kate.'

'Hello, David. Sticking with the French look tonight, then?'

'Moi? Yeah, I thought I'd keep it, just for tonight.'

'Good choice. It really suits you, shows off your cheekbones. Careful you don't cut your fingers on them. You should wear your hair like that more often . . .'

Was this a come on? Surely not . . . 'Um, thanks.'

'Nice party so far. It's been fun, hasn't it?'

'It has. In fact, it's been the best week of my life and I just want to say thanks. Thanks, Kate, for everything.'

'It's my pleasure, darling.'

I knew that Kate was just being theatrical calling me darling. It suited her, and I mean it nicely, in a good way. I couldn't help myself, though, I had to keep going, had to say something more when I really needed not to.

'No, honestly. I want to say thanks for so many things, for teaching me how best to learn my lines, for teaching me to hit my mark, for helping me understand how my character thinks. Thanks for not being cross when I come in too early before you've finished your line and thanks, thanks so much for not screaming too loudly when I crushed your foot when we did the dance scene on Wednesday. Really, thanks. Thanks a million.'

Kate edged away from me, slowly at first, then slightly quicker. Was that panic in her eyes or just Silk Cut smoke? 'Like I said, it was . . . fun.'

'There is *something* else.' That was not smoke – that was blind terror.

' . . . What?'

'Well, I was just . . . wondering . . .'

'What?' She was clearly looking for the nearest exit.

'I was just wondering if, you know, with this being a party and everything and your boyfriend not being here and me having played your boyfriend, well I just thought that maybe you'd like to, well, sort of fancy . . .'

'No.'

'No. Absolutely. Of course not. Silly of me to ask.'

'Yes. Bye, David. Enjoy the party.'

'Thanks. You too . . . look, no hard feelings?'

'I'm leaving.'

I knew that I'd go and bollocks it all up somewhere down the line.

9

Just Who Is The 5 O'Clock Hero?

I first heard 'Just Who Is The 5 O'Clock Hero?' on *The Gift*, as an album track, but it was released as an import on 11 June, 1982 and sold like a fire gone wild. If this record was a house, its occupants would be throwing children out of first-floor windows onto next door's mattresses. It went to number eight in the charts, the biggest selling import ever at that time. Again, I was more than happy to help put it there.

'Just Who Is The 5 O'Clock Hero?' is a prime example of The Jam's new-found direction. It's soulful and heartfelt. In later years I learned that Paul wanted it recorded much slower than this, but I don't care – I love it. The core message was aimed at Paul's support for the 'JOBS not YOPS' campaign. YOPS was an initiative to develop schemes for unemployed school leavers but there were no jobs for them to go to, nothing concrete. It was just a way to dress up figures for the government's own benefit. It was a completely detested scheme, not least by me. I had no plans to stay at school. As someone who wanted to put pen to paper for a living, I was stuffed. School wasn't giving me the experiences I needed to become a writer and I knew I'd never learn my trade in the system. Problem was, where *would* I learn it? No matter, right then – hair was a *much* more important item on my agenda.

Maybe it was the barber's shop back in Bridgford that was in my blood, maybe it was loving the way that Paul dressed and the way he wore his hair, maybe it was the attention to detail, the sharp suits which Dad had made for him, maybe it was the make-up from being in the musical, I don't know. What I do know, is that looking good for me – my clothes, my shoes, my hair – had become as much a priority for me as my music.

Mum told me that Paul's hair at that time was massive in 1967, the year I was born, so I went up to the attic to root amongst old suitcases, Christmas decorations and my old Meccano set. There, I found Dad's collection of *Hairdresser Monthly* magazines, which dated back to the late 1950s. Grampa Lines started saving them and passed them to Dad when he came out of the army and joined Grampa in the shop.

Some of the photos in them are just hilarious, with the models staring off at something fascinating in the middle distance. There was a man on page fifty-one of September 1966 with a huge beehive on his head and a droopy handlebar moustache. I didn't think that look would suit me.

It wasn't until February 1968 that I found what I was looking for. Danny Butto wrote about how some salons would actually iron your own hair for you. According to the magazine, this was the very best way to achieve super silky, poker-straight hair. The mods who were modelling this style had hair just like Paul's (although not as cool) and it seemed that if I followed the instructions, I may well finally get perfect Weller hair. So, where to start? What I needed to do was get hold of some greaseproof paper. This was very important, as it was to act as a barrier and protect my hair from the intense heat of the iron. It obviously did the trick, because the results shown in those pictures were the business. But ironing your own hair didn't seem like a particularly easy operation, I needed someone to help me. Somehow Dad wasn't my first choice.

'Hello?'

'Hi, Mrs Bowerman. It's David here. Is Rik there?'

I waited about two minutes before he managed to get from one end of the house to the other to reach the phone. I was surprised there wasn't one in each room. Someone should have invented a portable phone just for them.

'All right, Dave.'

'Skill, man. What are you doing after tea tonight?'

'Not much. Dinner's nearly ready, actually. Might have a couple of frames . . . fancy a game?'

'No, thanks. But I will come round. I want you to help me with something . . .'

Two hours later I was round at Rik's. 'What did you have for your tea?'

'We had coq au vin and chips for dinner. You?'

'Fish Finger sarnie, choc-ice then a Marlboro on the way over.'

'Nice. There's some freshly brewed coffee on. Want one?'

'Um, yeah . . . go on, then.'

'OK. Coming up. Anyway, what's this thing you want me to help you with?'

'I've made an important discovery. It's a hair thing.'

'A *hair thing*?'

'That's right, Rik. It'll give me the ultimate Weller look. Want to help me?'

'Sure, what do you want me to do?'

'I want you to help me iron my own hair . . .'

We did the deed in Rik's mum's utility room. We had a utility room at home, but we called it a kitchen. I set the ironing board up and Rik got the Morphy Richards out. It looked like something from *Star Wars*, with flashing lights, different dials and settings and a filter that did something to the water before it trickled inside. Ours had a hole in the top where we filled it from the tap. But the Bowermans' iron was something else, it might even have been self-cleaning, like their oven. In our house our oven was cleaned by Mum.

'Right, plug it in and switch the bugger on.'

'Have you ever done any ironing before, Rik?'

'No. We have someone who comes in and does that sort of thing for us. You?'

'Yeah. My mum.'

'There's all sorts of settings on this contraption. If we're not careful it might transport us back in time, Dave.'

'In that case, set the controls for 1967.'

'We've got silk, wool, synthetics and cotton. Which one do you think?'

'God, I'm not sure. Let's try cotton – after all, we don't want the thing too hot.'

'Good point. Steam?'

'Why not?'

'I can't find any greaseproof, Dave, but I have got a roll of cling-film.'

Even I knew that this was a stupid idea, trying to iron my hair through cling-film would make it melt and stick to me like glue and we'd be in a right, royal mess. Well, I would.

'Forget the plastic food wrap – it's a fucking disaster waiting to happen. This is my hair we're talking about and I'm not prepared to start cutting corners. Tear us a page out of the *NME*.'

'OK. Here we go. Now, bend down nice and slowly

and put your head on the ironing board . . .'

The staff nurses in the casualty department at St James's were incredibly helpful. They were overwhelmingly sympathetic and they'd all got incredible legs. According to the consultant it would take the best part of six weeks for the burns on the side of my scalp to heal and only then if I avoided washing my hair for the next twenty-one days. I had to apply cream every morning and then again before bed, plus, I had to avoid all contact with direct sunlight. The surgical gauze needed regular changing, there was a risk of infection and when I did eventually come to wash my poor hair I'd have to condition it with Lenor.

When Rik's mum dropped me off from hospital, my father was far from pleased. They had to chop out the damaged hair so they could treat the wound, but you couldn't see it because of all the bandages. Dad couldn't bear the sight of me and turned away. Mum followed him into the kitchen and I sat on the sofa whilst Chris and Phil almost pissed themselves laughing. Chris was purple in the face and Phil had to leave the room on all fours. There was some whispering from the kitchen and Dad reappeared.

'You'll need that hair seeing to. I can fix it for you. Oh, lad, you used to have such lovely hair. Wavy Davey, that's what we used to call you and Christ, just look at it now. You're an embarrassment, son. I suppose we'll just have to concentrate on your brothers and give you up as a bad job. Let's hope they don't get any stupid ideas like you – singing and dancing and writing poetry and ironing your hair. Do you want me to make you something like presentable again?' If he wanted to, I reckon Dad could have given me a short back and sides with his tongue.

It had been a month since *The Boy Friend* finished. I was on Main Street on a Saturday afternoon. The sun was out, the street deserted and I kept checking over my shoulder for that paper bag which was following Fiona and me on our way to the cricket pitch all that time ago. I was on my way to Lizzie's house to work on writing sketches for the end of year revue. There was a bag, but I was unsure if it was the same one. I decided not to confront it, just keep an eye on its movements.

I stopped outside Wide-a-Wake Records. A toddler in his pushchair sucked on a Milk Maid ice lolly. His huge mop of blond curls was so enormous it looked like he was wearing a comedy wig and his romper suit had a button badge pinned to it. My heart skipped a beat – it was exactly the same one that Paul wore, the Dennis the Menace one. The desire to own this badge was instantly intoxicating and there wasn't a soul around to stop me taking it from him. He wouldn't miss it – he probably didn't even know that he was wearing it. I looked up the street, and then I looked down. Nobody was watching – not even the paper bag which was being battered by the wind against the window of Jack Fulton's.

'Hello, little soldier.'

He opened his wide mouth, smiled, and a trickle of icy milk snaked down his chin. He giggled and kicked his feet and I ruffled his hair.

'That's a nice badge.'

It was a very nice badge and I wanted it for myself. I'd hunted high and low for one of those for months and there it was, mine for the taking. Like taking badges from a baby. Still nobody to be seen and I reached in and unclipped it. The child looked up at me and his bottom lip started to tremble. Suddenly, I was awash with guilt. As I tried to pin it back on the baby, the mother appeared from inside the shop. I dropped the badge on the pavement and scrambled to pick it up. 'I think he lost this,' I said.

'Thanks. Don't I know you?' she said.

I vaguely recognised her as the older sister of someone in my science group.

'You're him, from the play. You were brilliant – can I have your autograph, please?'

My guilt was drowning me. It was all that I could do to breathe. 'No, it's someone else. You must be mistaken.'

I handed her back the badge, pricking my thumb with the pin, before walking quickly down the road towards Lizzie's house.

10

The Bitterest Pill (I Ever Had To Swallow)

Paul wrote 'The Bitterest Pill' whilst on holiday in Italy in the early summer of 1982. When he came back from his break, he'd made some serious decisions, one of which was to record this and put it out as a single. It was a departure from the typical Jam sound and was battered black and blue by the critics. Hardly any guys liked it, in fact it was almost a girly Jam song, but I liked it because, once again, Paul was pushing himself, the band and me in new and exciting directions. Sure, there's a classic Jam sound but there's also the freshness of a new day when a fan comes across something challenging and bold – and this was it. Despite this thunderous U-turn in style, 'Bitterest Pill' went to number two in the charts, although this was probably due to the mighty Jam army keeping their collections up to date. I bought it because I really liked it. In fact, I'll stick my neck out and say it's in my top twenty Jam songs. There, I've said it.

The two tracks on the B-side of 'Bitterest Pill' weren't half bad, either. These were recorded, as was the A-side, in August 1982 at the Maison Rouge Studios in Fulham. My favourite out of 'Pity Poor Alfie' and the cover of Peggy Lee's 'Fever', was 'Alfie'. The horn section was supposedly nicked from the theme tune to *The Sweeney*, but I'm not sure about that myself. It certainly wasn't sampled although it may well have been an influence. Whatever; what I do know is that 'Bitterest Pill' reminds me of the trip which me and Rik took. Like Paul, we needed a holiday.

Studying for our O levels had been, for me at least, horrible. The only results I could be sure of were English and drama; assessed coursework to date meant that I couldn't fail. The other subjects – geography, maths, history, physics (actually, I could have been in with a chance on that one; I got ninety-nine per cent for a piece

I copied out of a book on astronomy) and RE – were anyone's guess. These subjects bored me to distraction; maybe that was the problem, I was too easily distracted. Not by the goings-on in class, but by a distant crow flapping effortlessly past the window – where was it going? Where'd it been? Clouds on the horizon took up my thoughts and clouded my brain, the sound of someone's chair scraping across the floor sounded like a sound effect off *Sound Affects*. Honestly, a pin dropping whisked me off to another world, my world, and there was nothing to convince me that it wasn't a better place than the school I was in. My heart wasn't in my exams. Looking back, my head was in the clouds – and I liked it up there. I thought I was above everything . . .

I only got two O levels: drama and English. The rest were all crappy CSEs. I did the best that I could, that much I do know. Mum and Dad were hugely supportive and all it meant was that I'd go into the sixth form and spend an extra year doing resits. In contrast, academia came easily to my brother Chris. His hand, his brain, he could turn them to anything and without effort. That Rubik's cube that he still carried everywhere with him, personified his brain – always turning, always analysing, always, always seeking out new angles. In a sense, I was exploring other avenues too – but for me it was a spiritual thing, a way of developing feelings. For Chris, it was about getting what he could out of the school system.

Chris was into music now, finding his own pop path. Not that I approved. It was the New Romantics he followed first. A natural artist and gifted cartoonist, Chris sailed through art and technical drawing. He didn't care for The Jam and I didn't care for his art school crap. We used to compete, across the upstairs landing. Chris with his floppy haircut and his drivel on his portable birthday tape deck, me with the mighty Jam on my bedroom stereo. There was always going to be one winner.

It was a given that Rik would gain top marks in everything. He sailed through his exams and got As and Bs in equal number. (Maybe I should backtrack and call this chapter 'David Watts'?) The song 'David Watts' was originally by The Kinks and The Jam covered it and then released it as a single back in 1978. It's about a school golden boy who excels at everything. I can remember sitting in my last exam, daydreaming, looking at Rik scribbling away whilst the lyrics to the song flowed through my mind.

That summer, a little way in through my studies for the retakes, we decided upon a cycling holiday, culminating in going to see The Jam, live in concert, at the Bridlington Spa Pavilion. A lot of my time had been spent plotting the trip, poring over maps and making mix-tapes for the journey instead of revising. I'd saved up pocket money for the holiday and Mum and Dad gave me some money as a present for agreeing to have another crack at my exams. I couldn't wait.

It was the first day of the journey and already the morning was wasted. Five minutes to eleven and I was ready to punch Rik's lights out. He was nearly two hours late for the arranged set-off time for our trip. Bastard. And, when he did eventually show, he was sporting his Secret Jam Shoes. Double bastard. Essentially they were a customised mod version of your basic cycling shoe, but he'd painted the black leather centre panel white, so it looked like a bowling shoe. It was unorthodox, but effective. This compounded my frustration at losing two hours' travelling time. Rik could both infuriate me and at the same time make me boil with jealousy.

We set off under an eel-grey sky riding two abreast,

me on my trusty BSA ten-speed and Rik on his Claude Butler Tour de France ultra-lightweight replica. My bike's weight handicap was increased even further by the ghetto blaster strapped to the top of my double panniers with a set of stripy, elastic crocodile clips. Unless I was very careful, it would fall off when I went too fast round a bend and there'd be no more Jam for the rest of the trip – what a terrifying thought that was.

It was all going well till about fifteen miles in. The breeze was gentle, the sun lurked behind low, dense cloud and the traffic was surprisingly light. Then, out of the blue, disaster struck and I made a discovery which was going to impact on the first stage and set us back considerably. I slammed on the brakes, skidded to a halt and turned the bike around. Rik pulled up and asked me what was wrong. 'Something serious has happened and I need to get back home urgently. You go ahead – I'll see you there.'

'What's so urgent?'

'I've only gone and forgotten the hairdryer . . .'

Rik talked me out of going back to Garforth. He was right – if we'd split up, then all kinds of difficulties could have arisen. Talking about it today, more than twenty years later, I'm not surprised at myself for wanting to go back for a hairdryer. Obsession with appearance ruled my life, and the horror of crap hair for one night, let alone one week, was unthinkable.

We decided to stop off en route at a Boots and get a little travel number. Job done, we arrived at the youth hostel in Helmsley at one minute to nine. We were exhausted, and headed straight for the showers then out to the pub. My hairdryer was pathetic and useless. I might as well have got Rik to blow on my head to dry it, it was that crap.

Next morning my head felt like a cow had shat in it. The monster session on Pernod and blacks had taken its toll. I lost count of how many we had. There had been no problem with getting served by the landlord. Perhaps it was because we were new faces, with different accents. It was a young pub on the whole, and lively, too. Back home, the only two pubs we could get served in were the Old George and the Bird in Hand. They simply asked you once what your age was, you said eighteen and that was that.

On top of the hangover we found that our daily chore was to mow the lawn. Not all youth hostels operated the chore system and I don't know now if any still do.

If the hostel you were staying in subscribed to the chore ethic, you'd hopefully get something easy to do – like running a duster down the banister rail or polishing the receiver on the public phone in the lobby – but mowing the lawn? I didn't think so. We decided to leg it but our plans came to nought when we found the bikes locked in the shed. It was impenetrable. There was no option but to get the Flymo out and get on with it. An hour later we were on our way.

Destination: Skipton. Another North Yorkshire market town, but much bigger and busier than Helmsley. Total travelling distance: fifty-four miles. It was a blisteringly hot day, and we spent most of the ride in tandem, discussing the merits of shaving our legs like Tour de France riders. I'd made a special Jam cycling compilation tape and it worked well with some ultra-fast tracks at breakneck speed and then some slow ones mixed in. Their mood captured perfectly our terrain and somehow seemed to lift the countryside as we pedalled through it. The stench from the fertiliser that mixed with the fumes from passing cars seemed sweeter as we cycled through them; Paul's voice spurred me along.

First stop was the Skipton branch of Boots where

we purchased a pair of leg-waxing kits. We had lunch in an old-fashioned pub and were pleased to find it equipped with a fantastic jukebox as well as a pool table. Rik trounced me four games to one but I put that down to being distracted by his cycling shoes.

We checked into the hostel, delighted to find a party of Italian sixth-form schoolgirls were also staying. We set about waxing each other's legs (me and Rik, sadly, not me and the jaw-droppingly stylish and sexy Italian bombshells). The pain was like pain I'd never known before but I got my revenge on Rik for not tipping me off on making shoes like his by tearing the strip off his shin with great ferocity. I also made a mental note to do his absurd moustache one night whilst he was asleep. Shoes were my thing, not his.

Into the shower, feather-cut teased, on with the white 501s and then out into town. We visited a couple of pubs that were full of farmers harping on about the harvest. Sticking a record on the jukebox was clearly a hanging offence so we moved on to a younger pub and found it full of younger farmers all harping on about the harvest. We played some more pool and ended up playing doubles with a couple of Worzel Gummidge types in their early twenties. When we told them we were en route to see The Jam they told us about the time that Smokie came to Skipton. Rik drank three pints of cider and told them that back home he'd got a brand new combine harvester and he'd happily give them the key. They, equally happily, gave Rik a black eye and we got out of there sharpish.

That night I hardly slept a wink – not just because of the Kiwi backpacker on the bunk below who must have been captain of the Under 21s All Black Olympic Wanking Team – and who spent the entire night practising – but because the next day we set sail for Bridlington – to go and see The Jam! This was our first ever Jam concert and we were up most of the night talking about what we thought it would be like. It was a great distraction, being away from home, not thinking about revising again, instead getting worked up about Weller, Buckler and Foxton in the flesh. What would they play? Who was the support? Did I care? Would we get near the front? What would Paul be wearing? Tomorrow we were going to see The Jam – live!

We were up with the lark, and got off lightly with the hostel chore which was to Hoover the lounge. We were away by eight-thirty on the long and winding road to Bridlington, seaside Mecca of the North. It was a sixty-three-mile journey, but the feverish excitement building up inside us at the prospect of seeing Paul in a few hours' time drove us along at a furious pace and after just two and a half hours of serious non-stop pedalling we pulled into the seaside town in perfect time for an early lunch. I was knackered.

Fish and chips on the pier, scooters everywhere. Harrington jackets and fishtail parkas, button badges and bowling shoes, Jam shoes, white socks, Crombies and crew cuts stared back from every corner. Candy floss and Kiss-Me-Quick hats. It was straight out of *Quadrophenia*, and I jumped up onto the harbour wall and looked out to sea to watch the gulls following the trawler and the light on the silvery water and I turned and looked in, out over the sea of green parkas and scooters and smoke and I closed my eyes very slowly, storing the scene away in the back of my mind and climbed back down. This felt like a dream that I dreamed a thousand times before.

The hostel didn't open till four, so we went to a Spar and bought a bottle of vodka and a carton of orange and pegged out in the grounds, dozing under a willow tree talking about the night and how it'd really feel to see them in the flesh after so long. I felt like I was going to meet my maker – I was *nervous* about seeing Paul. The vodka numbed me nicely, the slight afternoon sun warmed my face. That, and all the cycling, made me drift away to sleep.

I was dreaming I was riding my bicycle, at night, down a never-ending country lane which was lit only by the light of the moon. It was the height of midsummer and the midnight air lay heady with night-scented stock. I pedalled gently away and as I turned a corner the path turned into a great, long moonbeam which stretched away, far over the fields and arched up, up into the night sky and led all the way through the tiny clouds to the bright and distant moon.

The moonbeam twinkled with space dust and in the distance someone sang a song. I steered the machine onto the moonbeam and we travelled towards the planet and slowly, very slowly, I felt myself leaving the ground. It felt so real, I really was flying. I looked down and suddenly it wasn't my bike any more, it was a Lambretta. I was riding a very special Lambretta – it had magic pedals like a bicycle and I saw twenty of my faces beaming back at me from the twenty chrome mirrors and the higher we flew, the brighter the stars shone.

I was so high above the fields and it felt like I could reach out and lick the moon. There was a man on the moon. He stood on the far side and it was he who was singing. He walked towards me and stretched out his hand and beckoned me to go to him and my legs were going like pistons and there was laughter in the air and I stood up in my seat to exert more power and I was almost there, I was almost there! Just as I got to him, just as he reached out his hand, the laughter became almost hysterical and it snapped me out of my dream and I sat bolt upright, opened my eyes and there were the beautiful Italian sixth-formers.

They pointed at me, laughing like Venetian drains. Two of them had found me being asleep so hilarious that they were on their hands and knees and banging their fists on the ground. What was so funny? Oh, then I saw. No wonder the dream felt so real – for however long I'd been asleep on the grass I'd been pedalling like crazy with my legs in the air. I must have looked a right prize prick. They pointed and screamed at me – '*Il che morindo mosca! Il che morindo mosca!*' I hadn't a clue what they were on about and I certainly didn't want to know, so I just waved back like some grinning idiot and sloped off to check in. I got into the shower and washed off my embarrassment. I watched it dripping off me and down the plughole and I wondered when I'd finally manage just a degree of cool. The only saving grace was that Rik wasn't there to witness it; he'd gone off to buy pork scratchings.

We only had three hours to go till The Jam were on stage. I'd done good work on my feather-cut and had opted for white 501s, black Lonsdale t-shirt and my navy and white bowling shoes. Pubs were packed with fans before the gig, everywhere was pretty much elbow-room only and we ended up in some place called the Admiral Nelson, standing at the bar getting just nicely pissed on rum and Coke. Again, there was no problem getting served – half the kids in there looked younger than I did. There was no chance of a police raid – it was so packed they wouldn't even have got through the door. I wasn't going to go too mad with the drink before the gig – I'd waited so long for that moment, I wanted to remember every single detail for every day of my life. We supped up our rum and headed for the venue. I literally had to stop myself from skipping down the street.

We were early, it didn't start for almost an hour, but it didn't matter because we wanted to get in and get right down the front. Outside, in the queue, I overheard snippets of conversation from fellow fans and I was struck by the variety of different accents: Geordies, Yorkshire, Scouse, Mancunian, even Welsh. They were all talking about roughly the same thing – will they have the electric acoustics out for 'Entertainment', will they play this, will they play that. Someone was banging on about what a 'frigging great scrap' his lot – 'The Cross Gates Stylists' – had with 'The Kippax Casuals' at a previous gig on this tour earlier in the week. I didn't fucking get it, and I still don't – mods fighting other mods? What was the point in that? It was a touch intimidating, being in the middle of all that aggression, but somehow it all added to the electric night through which I fizzed.

Getting inside the Pavilion was like stepping into a furnace. The floor swam in warm beer and the air was thick with smoke. The noise from the chanting, baying crowd drowned out the support act – a skinhead poet who went by the name of Seething Wells. I could hardly believe it, I mean, putting on a poet to entertain The Jam Army? Then I got it. I got it right there and then what Paul was trying to do. He could have stuck anyone on as support and they wouldn't have survived the audience who were so desperate to see The Jam they would have even booed The Beatles off stage. Paul was also trying to make his audience see that by having someone as support come on and recite poetry, he was distancing himself from the 'Jam Army'. Seething Wells, however, was on fire. I don't mean he was on top form, I mean the man had been *set alight*. The record company were handing out album sleeves on the way in, and someone had set fire to one and sent it, flaming, spinning through the air, skimming the heads of the crowd like a fiery frisbee onto the stage where it caught the sleeve of his green bomber jacket and in precisely three seconds flat the thing went up like a bonfire. Seething was seriously seething and frantically tried to get his jacket off but it had started melting into him, a roadie ran on with a bucket of water and chucked it all over the poor fat poet and then Seething ran off – it was like a trip to the fucking circus – and then, from nowhere, John, Paul's dad, was on stage and a mighty, mighty cheer went up . . . 'For those of you sitting down at the back, please be upstanding for . . . The Jam!' The place exploded.

We were as close to the stage as we could get without being crushed to death. I was in prime position in front of Paul's mike stand and they opened with 'The Eton Rifles' and I was lost in the crowd as we moved together, heaving, swaying, jumping as one. The feeling of togetherness, the feeling of coming together with thousands to become one was . . . religious. I looked over at Rik, looked down and saw that his Special Jam Shoes were completely cabbaged from the trampling. He didn't care, and I certainly didn't care, because it was like I'd lived all my life for that moment and there, in the middle of all of those strangers, those lifelong friends, in front of my god, I was reborn.

The Jam played every song I could wish for. There was something from every album and one number I'd never heard before. Even though I loved the show, I hated it in parts. I hated it every time the band stopped playing, not because there was no music, but because the mod army struck up and they chanted away like football hooligans and they weren't here like I was, for Paul, they might as well have been Chelsea away to Sunderland as far as I was concerned.

It had been a glorious set. That's right, glory was what I saw in Paul's face that night. And maybe just a hint of desperation, but he must have been shagged out

– I had no idea just how energetic it would all be. After the encore, when they played 'Little Boy Soldiers', 'Butterfly Collector' and 'When You're Young', the emotion swelled in my stomach and tears rushed down my face and the joy washed over me and it felt like I was being bathed, baptised maybe, but then I realised some twat had spilled his pint down my neck.

Afterwards, we hung around backstage for a while but there was no sign of anyone coming out. 'Bugger. I wanted to get Paul to sign my shoelace.' Rik'd got a shoelace which he said came off the stage and swore was Paul's. I hadn't got the heart to tell him that Paul was wearing white loafers, and just beamed back at him as he waved it under my nose.

We got talking to a mod from Macclesfield who told us he very nearly didn't make it to see them because the exhaust fell off his scooter halfway down the motorway. He asked us if we came on our bikes as well. 'Yes, brother, but we don't tend to get those kind of hiccups with a ten-speed racer.' He cleared off and we found an off-licence and bought four cans of Tetley's and half a bottle of Lamb's Navy Rum and sat under the cloudy black night beneath the branches of an oak in the hostel garden and we talked about the gig for hours, not that we could hear what either of us was talking about because we both had tinnitus.

We didn't get in, the manager had locked up at midnight and the bell wasn't working but we didn't mind, we slept under the stars. In the morning, we packed slowly and quietly, exhausted from it all. I'd got a crick in my neck which felt like someone had taken an axe to it. We were to set off after breakfast on the first homeward leg of the trip. We got the AA road atlas out and opened it up over the hostel kitchen table. Rik looked deep in thought as he studied it. 'Right, Dave. Where are we going?'

I don't think, today, twenty years later, that having your life mapped out for you is a good thing. In fact, I think it's the worst thing you could wish for. It's far from realistic, it's limiting, it narrows your life in *every* way and, back then, I didn't have a clue where I was going. All I knew was that I wanted to write, or at least try and write. Rik was going to work in the bank with his dad or be a brewer. He had it all mapped out. 'I don't know, Rik,' I said. 'You decide.'

I felt let down by something; I didn't know what and I didn't know why. It annoyed me and I finally thought it was because I'd expected Paul, Bruce and Rick to smile a bit more. I knew it was stupid of me, but I just wanted them to look like they were enjoying it as much as I had. Maybe the urge to go and see The Jam wasn't just about seeing The Jam. Maybe it was about escape more than anything else. About getting out of Garforth under my own steam, not sitting on a train or in a car or a plane or getting a bus out of there. I think physically *propelling* myself out of the place was the point. Perhaps it was some sort of primal urge, probably sexual in origin, I don't know.

We set off for Scarborough, Rik still in his Jam shoes and the wind was in our hair and we simply bowled along. I played the gig over in my head and it dawned on me that Bruce and Rick weren't simply Paul's backing band. Something happened when the three of them played together, some immense chemistry. There was an energy all of its own, a fire that burned so bright inside all three of them and I guessed that, like me, they must have been lost in the music that night. The power and the glory of The Jam, the raw balls of the music didn't come from one man alone – it came from all three. The Jam were three people and always would be, forever and ever, amen.

We stopped cycling after an hour. Rik needed the

loo and had to nip over a dry-stone wall. I thought he just needed a piss: 'I haven't got any paper, Dave. Go and buy a hot dog from that burger van – he's bound to give you a serviette.' I did as I was told and the man in the van handed me a stinking, tepid brown log in a stale bridge roll, squirted red sauce on and wrapped it in a serviette. I walked back, across the deserted Dales road and handed Rik his dog over the top of the wall. 'There's no onions, Dave.' There's gratitude for you. After Rik finished we took off on our bikes. We arrived in Scarborough late in the afternoon. The sun shimmered on the road and bounced like sparks off my spokes as we coasted down the coast road and into the hostel. The manager was unlocking the door, just opening up. We were surprised, to say the least, to find him in full make-up, a slinky little black cocktail dress and high, strappy heels. Turned out he was an amateur dramatics enthusiast and was understudying the mother in *A Taste Of Honey*. The girl who was due to play her pulled out due to water retention.

I'd quite like to have gone, to see more theatre, but Rik wanted to go and check out the pubs on the seafront so after I'd showered and dealt with my hair that's what we did. I was waiting for Rik in the lobby and the phone was free. I hadn't planned it, but I stuck ten pence in and phoned home. 'Hi, Mum. It's me . . .'

'Oh, hello David. Thanks for ringing – we were all getting quite worried about you.'

'Sorry, but the queues for the phone have been about two miles long every night. It's taken me more than an hour to wait for this one.'

'I'm just glad that you're safe. You are safe, aren't you?'

'I am, I'm very safe. Last night's gig was just brilliant – I really enjoyed myself. Is everyone OK there?'

'We're well. Are you eating properly?'

'Certainly am. The fish and chips are terrific.'

'That's good, because you've got to keep your energy up on those long rides.'

'Don't worry – I will.'

'Good boy. I've got to go – there's cod for tea and I think the bag's boiled dry.'

'OK. Bye. Lots of love to everyone.' And I placed the receiver back down in its cracked, black Bakelite cradle and sat down on the step and thought about home. I missed my family. From the moment we walked into the nearest pub I knew I was going to get properly hammered. I ordered Scotch, for no other reason than Grampa Lines used to drink it. I remember wondering whether we drank Scotch for the same reason: to escape.

The next morning we were bound for Whitby, home of Captain Cook. Well, it would be if he weren't dead. Rik wanted to know why I'd got so pissed the previous night.

'Because we're on holiday, right?'

'Yeah, but that was a bit spooky.'

'My head hurts. It feels like some twat's camping in there.' We left it at that. I didn't tell him about missing Mum and Dad and Chris and Phil. Why couldn't I tell him things like that? We just left it at that.

On the way to Whitby I got a puncture. The tyre burst and I hurtled down a hill with a one-in-four gradient and articulated lorries crashed past me, just millimetres away. I struggled to stop the bike from falling over and I just about managed it, but not without spraining my ankle slightly as I instinctively put my foot down to stop it. There was a small hamlet signposted half a mile away, so we pushed the bikes there to change the inner tube, get out of the traffic and grab something for lunch. I must have been getting old . . . I never knew that a cheese ploughman's could ever cheer me up so much.

We sat outside on the bench and I sipped my lime and soda (very refreshing) and we watched the starlings as they settled on the telegraph wires. The sun threatened to come out and for a moment, just a moment, I forgot about revision and retakes and choices and decisions and it was just . . . like the way being on holiday should feel. Two cyclists came into view. Distant dots on the horizon,they reminded me of the entrance which Omar Sharif made on his horse in *Lawrence Of Arabia*. I pointed it out to Rik and he said he hadn't seen it because he didn't like Westerns.

They were laden with kit and as they pulled up in front of us we heard American accents. Those guys were fun. Danny and Jon introduced themselves – they had recently finished a spell in the military and were in England as part of their European cycling holiday which would take them through Spain, France and Italy, as well as Scotland, as they both had ancestors who were married to Robert the Bruce's cleaning lady, or something like that. We got talking about their amazing bikes which were built out of the same stuff they made the space shuttle from and could withstand temperatures so great they could cycle over the surface of the sun if they wanted to. They were about ten years older than us. I liked them. They were on their way to Whitby, because Danny's great-great-great-grandmother chopped down some of the trees which they built the bow of *The Mayflower* with, or so he'd been told. Jon asked me why I'd got such a huge ghetto blaster strapped to my bike, when a Walkman would be better. I told him I'd no idea what he was on about and he got his out – it was so tiny. He strapped it to my shorts, put the little headphones on and pressed play – it was unbearable. It was a band called The Doors and the singer sounded like he didn't mean a word he was singing. When I asked Jon if Hinge and Bracket supported them he just stared back at me from behind these blue, plastic cycling goggles. I'd never seen anything so ridiculous in my life – he looked like a spaceman.

We cycled on together, the four of us, en route to Whitby. When we arrived, we checked in and Danny made us a drink which NASA sent into space with the shuttle crews, you rehydrated it and it bubbled and fizzed and looked amazingly brightly orange and generally, we told them, tasted like tramp's piss. Kia-Ora was a hundred times better.

We decided on an early tea at a pub up the road, and Danny went to the bar because next to them, we were looking much younger. We all had beer, because that's what Danny wanted and he had a cheese ploughman's because I told him I'd had one and he liked the name.

We'd finished eating, and I was talking about The Jam. They'd never heard of them, and I was trying to explain what they were, how they sounded, when in walked a girl. I can see her now like it was yesterday. She walked up to the bar, ordered half a lager and lime in a broad, New York accent and sat down on a stool. She'd got masses of corkscrew hair that was a rich, reddish blonde and she wore a floaty sarong which revealed long, freckly legs as she crossed and uncrossed them on her stool. Her scoopy-necked t-shirt had a packet of fags tucked under her sleeve and she wore bits of coloured braid tied around her wrists and pretty ankles. She looked arty, and she reminded me of Kate. I made a mental note to send her a post-card the next day. Danny sidled over, said hello and asked her if she'd like to join her fellow Americans for a drink. She did. Her name was Maria, she was an artist and as soon as she sat down the dynamic between us four new friends changed in the bat of just one eyelid.

Her bright, green eyes and wide, white smile had us eating out of the palm of her delicate hand in seconds. Her chest rose and fell tantalisingly as she talked, and as she spoke, she'd touch each of us in turn on the arm. Maria was very sophisticated, older than me and Rik, but younger than Danny and Jon. I couldn't take my eyes off her. She told us that she was staying in a hotel in Whitby because she was here for inspiration to paint coastal scenes for her next exhibition. Apparently, her great-great-uncle used to stop off here and buy his kippers whilst sailing twice around the world on a bread board, or something. That was the first time I saw the presence of a single woman come between friends. I remember being jealous of the power which she held, the power to make people like her.

After half an hour me and Rik were feeling decidedly left out of things, so we got out of there and left the three of them to it. The atmosphere had turned nastily competitive between the four of us and I didn't care for it. It wasn't the competition, it was the feeling I got that it would end in tears. I made some excuse about having to phone home and Rik came with me.

We went and sat in the pub next door, played some pool and stuck some Jam on the jukebox. I didn't feel bad about leaving, it was cool just being alone with Rik again.

Next morning, at breakfast, we saw Danny and Jon. They were laughing to themselves and looking very pleased and when I asked them if they'd had a good night they said that they most certainly did and winked at each other.

That night was the last night of our trip. We were going to be staying in the ancient, walled City of York. We swapped addresses with Danny and Jon and promised to keep in touch. Jon said that they might go to York because his cousin's wife's great-great-grandfather once baked Richard III some scones there, and he accidentally burnt them and at the moment Richard bit into one, someone shot him in the eye with an arrow and he turned him into a pillar of salt, or something like that.

The sunshine was not nearly so bright that day, and the breeze which came with the gathering clouds was a bitter one. We cycled straight into the centre of York and got to a baker's where we bought sausage rolls, sarnies, vanilla slices and refreshing drinks. We took them down to the river, the mighty River Ouse which cleaves its way through the heart of the place, and sat next to it on the steps. There were hundreds of tourists out on the water, and we watched a Viking longboat cruise past with a full crew of re-enactment types aboard, getting ready for some good old rape and pillage.

We fed the ducks and talked about what we were going to do when we'd got through sixth form. Rik talked about a life in brewing – or in banking which his dad could arrange. I told him that I wanted to be a writer and he almost choked on his Um Bongo. This was a moment not without intimacy, drenched in years of bristling friendship, and I did not want it to end. But that moment did feel like the beginning of the end of something. Overhead, the sky blackened a little and with it came goose pimples up and down my spine and my neck and my thin, willowy arms.

We resolved to make it a last night to remember, and agreed on trying to get into a club once the pubs shut. I bought a postcard for Kate, told her I'd had a great little holiday, went to a mind-blowing Jam gig and that I couldn't wait to see her when I got home.

I stuck a first class stamp on it and slipped it into a postbox. It was freshly painted, and I got a red splodge on my fingernail. It looked pretty so I let it dry. It was like a receipt for the card for Kate.

We had tea, chicken supreme that was far from supreme, and then we did our hair, got changed and then went out for our final drinking session of our short break. We walked through the funny little snickleways and ginnels, up and down the cobbled Shambles and then we found a funky-looking wine bar hidden away, called Oscar's. It had a tiled terrace, and we sat outside on it in our shades, drinking wine and smoking cigarettes and trying to look cool.

We talked about our trip and agreed it'd been brilliant. We said that at some point in the future we'd go on a scootering holiday – to another country. We talked about Maria, the American artist, and wondered whether or not American girls did it differently to English girls. As neither of us had actually done it then, we spoke with some authority, obviously, and concluded that they must do. Especially Californians. Because they're all blonde.

We ended up in a club called the Underground. It said on the sign outside that it used to be an ancient debtor's gaol, and the steps down to it were steep, wet and winding. The walls were dark and it was deliciously seedy. Lots of students in there, as well as a good smattering of slightly older people, plenty in their twenties who looked like they went out to work.

I was struck by the number of single girls, out for the night in groups. It was a good place, apart from the DJ, who played far too much Duran and Spandau for my liking. I got a rum and Coke and walked up to the booth and asked him for some Jam. He said no problem and then only went and played vile Haircut One Hundred's 'Love Plus One'. I *loathed* Haircut One Hundred.

I still do, come to think of it.

I spent the next half-hour plucking up courage to go over and talk to an attractive pair of girls in their rara skirts. They looked like they were in their early twenties. One of them was the spitting image of Kim Wilde. I asked if I could buy her a drink and she only went and said yes. You could have knocked me down with her feather boa.

We got talking, and it turned out that her and her mate Alison were both recently officially single and out for the night to celebrate their divorces which had just come through. I told her again that she looked like Kim Wilde and she told me that everyone said that. She was wearing so much lip gloss I could see my reflection in her lips. Kim's real name was Trace, and she said that her two children now lived in Florida with her ex-husband. She told me that she missed them so much, thought of them every day. 'Ah,' I said, 'they're the kids in America, then.' Suddenly she got something in her eye and ran off to the loo. I was kicking myself. Why did I try to be clever when I was clearly an idiot? I could have been well in there . . .

We had a few more drinks and then the DJ played 'Malice' for me. There was no sign of Kim/Trace and we got up and had a dance, which was basically me and Rik leaping around and pretending to play guitar like Paul, surrounded by loads of girls dancing around their handbags. At exactly the right moment I executed a perfect scissor-kick just after the bass break, but sadly ruined it by colliding with a pretty Claire Grogan-type dancing next to me. Her and the contents of her handbag spilled out over the floor and Rik and I decided to call it a night and sloped off in search of a kebab.

I was up half that night with violent food poisoning. The next morning I was excused duties due to illness, and it was down to Rik to clean the toilets. I didn't envy him. Not for one moment did I envy him. I could actually hear him *weeping* in there.

Rik didn't speak to me for the rest of that morning. We got our kit together without saying a word, we packed with pursed lips and set off for home in silence. It was an ill wind which blew us back to Garforth and that wasn't just down to the previous night's lamb and pitta bread combo. We hardly even spoke cycling back, and after an hour the rain clouds came together to black out what little light was left in the sad and seething sky. Overhead, the gods rumbled their disdain, and in the far distance lightning forks flicked through the charcoal sky to make the hairs on my neck stand up and twitch and twist like one thousand volts ran through each and every one. The air was heavy with resentment. It was going to take a storm of biblical proportions to clear the air that sad and sorry day.

All the way home we were buzzed by cars and thunking great juggernauts, motorcycles and even a small posse of parka'd-up scooterists buzzed us on the Tadcaster slip road. I could feel a migraine building behind my right eye and my neck had begun to grow numb. Breathing had become difficult. When we were almost home, Rik peeled off as he wanted to call in and have a cup of tea for ten minutes with his gran who lived around the corner. He'd promised his parents he would, he said.

I waved goodbye and carried on on my own. I wasn't feeling at all good, now. My tongue felt too big for my mouth and my throat felt like it was lined with sand-paper. I needed a drink. I stopped at a newsagent's about a mile from home, slung the bike down and headed straight for the fridge.

I grabbed the first can I could, tore open the ring pull and as I glugged the drink down, my eyes fell onto the magazine rack. My heart turned black. I was in a dream, I had to be dreaming . . .

The drink went down like I was swallowing a fistful of hatpins and my skull felt like someone had brought down a shovel on the back of it. I had to steady myself against the news-stand. My eyes, my brain, my soul, they simply could not comprehend the headline that I was reading. The front page of the *NME* read: 'Paul Weller Splits The Jam'. Blood gushed from my nostrils and both my legs gave way, as if viciously kicked from behind. Mist swirled in front of my eyes and as I went down, my head bounced back off the floor. My world, effectively, had drawn to a terrible, wretched close.

I came to in the storeroom of the shop with a bruise on my forehead the size of a football and the first thing that I saw was a mad hag wafting smelling salts under my nose. She was the spitting image of Fagin and had the devil's breath to match. I can smell it today, just writing this.

I paid for that copy of the *NME* with coins stained red with my own wet blood. Sitting outside the shop on the wall, I tried to read the article. I read it and reread it yet still it made no sense to me. I'd just seen them! How could he do this to me? I couldn't take in what the paper said, the words were just a jumbled mess in front of me. I was feeling sicker and sicker, I couldn't have felt any more ill but I had to get home. Cycling wasn't an option, I just leant on the bike and, slumped over the crossbar, I half pushed the bike home.

I half opened the back door to the house and collapsed through it onto the kitchen floor. Mum rushed up to me and scraped me into her arms. 'My poor boy!' I couldn't speak. I was in and out of reality, spinning between consciousness and unconsciousness and through the blur of steaming saucepans Mum took my hand. 'Here you are! Welcome home!' I managed, just managed, to get my words out. 'It's The Jam – they've split up.' And with that, I passed out again.

Looking back, I'm sure that the horrific news impacted on my illness. I had glandular fever, and it was a terrible, terrible case of it. I am convinced that my body went into shock at the break-up, even though I still didn't believe it. There had to be a mistake, there *had* to be. My fever meant that I could not speak – if I could have done, I'd have phoned the *NME* to check that the story was straight. The Jam had been not just my band, but my way of life and as I lay in my festering bed for two long months, sucking on ice cubes, I could see no reason ever to leave it again.

One day, in the boiling heat of my fever when I was clearly delirious, I almost lost my life. As I tossed and writhed in my bed, images of The Jam at Bridlington, Paul staring down at me from my bedroom wall, the exam results slip, Dad's face, Rik's face, Kate's face, swam in front of me, all laughing at me at once, like I was staring down some sickly kaleidoscope. It all became too much and I had to get out of the bed, out of the room, out of the house. I had no idea what I was doing, stumbling blindly about my room, thrashing out at the faces, covering my ears to drown out the taunting laughter. I crashed onto the landing and into Chris and Phil's room yet still they pursued me. Air. I needed air. I flung open the big double window and stuck my head out of it and gulped down the freshness which stung my lungs and down came a mist, a thick, swirling fog inside my mind. I hated Paul Weller more than anyone, then. He could piss off in a bin liner for all that I cared that day. I felt cheated, The Jam were my suit of armour – they gave me strength and focus and now he'd done it, he'd gone and spoiled everything. He said that he wanted them to mean something, to finish with dignity and that was all very well and good but what about me? If he was going to end it, then so was I.

The cool breeze brought me to my senses. If the wind hadn't picked up I doubt if I'd be telling this tale today. Maybe I'd been sleepwalking, maybe I meant to do it, I don't know, but I suddenly found myself standing, naked, on the window ledge. The sweat dripped down my forehead, onto my nose and onto my prick and very carefully, very frightened, I climbed back inside the room. In the garden below, I saw the cat watching me whilst he licked his paws.

As the days went by the fever passed, and I found the strength to wash my hair again. I simply still could not get over what Paul had done. What the fuck was he going to do with the rest of his life? He was only twenty-four for Christ's sake. If he hated being in The Jam that much, why not take a really long holiday and come back to it fresh? His dad must have been furious with him – after all, he'd put him out of a job as well as Bruce and Rick.

My dad tried to make things better for me. We were sitting in the garden, talking and smoking. It was my first cigarette since I'd got better and the first couple of drags on it sent me dizzy. 'I know how upset you must be, lad. What with your band splitting up and having to do your exams again.'

'Do you?'

'I think so. I also think I've got something which might help. If you want.'

'What, Dad?'

'Two words: Frank Sinatra . . .'

Dear God. 'What about the fat crook?'

'He might just fill the gap for you, you know. He's a very talented singer and I've always liked him. I thought if you gave him a real listen you would, too.

He might not be so . . . much of a disruptive influence, he might help you revise for your resits.'

'Thanks. I'll take Frank on board.'

'Good lad. Now, let's go inside and watch *Last Of The Summer Wine*. It's starting in a bit.'

'All right, Dad. I'll follow you in when I've finished this smoke.'

Give me strength, I thought.

I did follow Dad inside, but not to watch the codgers dicking around in the Dales. I walked up the stairs to my room and took a long hard look around it. I sat down in the middle of the bed and crossed my legs and I stared at the four walls and everywhere I looked, Paul's face stared right back at me. I went down to the kitchen, got a black bag and then I took down every poster, every picture, every interview, every poem I ever wrote but never sent and I filled the bag till it was fit to burst.

Paul had written my life for me. He'd sung songs about my mum and my dad, about my brothers Chris and Phil, about my aunties and uncles, about my grandparents, about my friends and our neighbours. He sung about the man who delivered our milk, the man who owned the shop on the corner and the people who bought their daily bread from him. He knew me and I knew Paul – or rather I thought I did. Weller was as much a part of my world as I was, but he wasn't there to share it any more. I picked up the bag, went out onto the landing and down the stairs, through the hall and out through the kitchen into the garden.

I sat down on the rockery and looked at the bag. The air was still and fresh and whilst I was indoors a thunderstorm came, tipped it down and left as quickly as it arrived. The skies were blue again, and the smell of wet moss filled my nose. I saw a raindrop on a leaf and watched a ladybird as it paddled in it like a pool. I stood up, walked to the garden shed and fetched a box of Swan Vestas, then emptied The Jam into the incinerator. I took out a match, struck it and lowered it inside and then I set fire to Paul Weller's face.

It burned quickly, the flame licking around his hair. He wasn't laughing at me now. I could hear him screaming as the fire whipped down his neck and onto his body, his clothes crumpling under the flame and then, with a whumpf, the whole lot went up with every cutting, every picture, my whole Weller archive burning out forever in a blaze of glory; my glorious revenge. I bent down, untied my bowling shoes, took them off one by one and dropped them deep into the heart of the roaring furnace. I took off my Lonsdale t-shirt and draped it, like a flag over a coffin, across the top of the incinerator. It sagged under the intense heat, and sighed, like it was breathing its last.

There was so much dense smoke from all of the paper that I had to stand back, quickly, as it belched up into my face. My eyes stung as much from crying as from the smoke and I placed the lid onto the bonfire and stood back to watch the bluey, dove-grey plumes coil up, out of the funnel and away through the branches of the silver birch. Hundreds of thousands of tiny black wafers of burnt paper floated up into the sky, propelled by the raw heat beneath and were carried away, dancing high over the garden fences of Garforth. I watched till the fire burned itself out and then I stood back. 'Goodbye, Paul.' I walked calmly back inside and ran myself a bath. I needed to make myself feel clean again.

11

Speak Like A Child

Going back to school for my retakes was like sitting down and having to eat a very large shit sandwich. Whereas before I was regarded as the cool mod, now I was looked upon as the school retard. Or that's what it felt like to me. I'd been in the sixth form for months but still it didn't feel right for me.

If I was worried about sixth form, it was nothing compared to how worried Dad had become about what had happened to Shergar. That horse had made him big money in the 1981 Derby, and when the prize stallion had been kidnapped from his stables in County Kildare,

Dad's world fell through the seat of his pants like mine did when The Jam split. We were both lost souls, thrown together by grief, a shared and desolate grief. 'Shergar the Wonder Horse' had been valued at £10 million, was named European Horse of the Year in 1981 and was retired from racing that September. Then he was kidnapped two years later, the year I took resits, and his capture entirely obsessed my dad, but my loss was the greater, believe me.

Dad pored over the papers whilst I mourned for The Jam. Apart from the football pools, Dad had never been a betting man but he had a love for Shergar. He kind of turned himself into a private eye and was always trying to solve the mystery for himself. 'It's the IRA. I'm telling you, lad, there'll be a ransom note before too long – they need the money for the machine guns . . .'

Being back at school taught me what to think, not how to think. I was suffocating, lost forever in my own self-doubt and with no direction, no motivation, devoid of all inspiration. The one plus was the social side, and it went some little way to counteract my embarrassment at resitting O levels whilst everyone else was marching up the academic ladder doing their A levels.

I was only too aware of my past failure. It didn't help that Rik had secured himself a mighty ten O levels, all top-flight grades, with little or no revision. 'I put it all down to the snooker, Dave – helps focus the mind – makes you see things from all the different angles. I think you just went in-off the black, that's all . . . you were unfortunate.'

I didn't know it at the time, but my misfortune was to shape my destiny.

I would put on a brave face before school each morning, and wear it like a mask. I kept it in my bedroom, on top of the dresser next to my hairdryer, and would put it on before I went down to breakfast. I was in classes with people I didn't know, people I didn't particularly like and I was studying things that didn't interest me. Drama and English were the only subjects that I held dear, and once I'd got those under my belt everything else just went in one ear and straight out the other. The days without Paul were empty and long and only added to my sad and lonely time at school. I couldn't help wondering what he was up to with his time now there was no more Jam. What was Paul *doing* all day long?

I was seeing less and less of Rik now that we were

in different sets and I'm sure this added to my turning into a right morbid bugger. I decided to find a replacement for The Jam – a new group for me to follow.

It was a short-lived project – there was nothing out there to touch what had gone. All there was, was a bunch of foppish limp-wristed fucks with zero talent, no dress sense and no emotion. They meant absolutely one hundred per cent nothing. Who was out there? That tosser Martin Fry? Wanking around in his gold lamé jacket and floppy fringe? He wasn't fit to breathe the same air as Paul Weller. Simon le Bon? Ponce. Marilyn? No thanks. David Bowie? Never wrote a half-decent tune in his life. Phil Collins? Looks like a bin man. Men at Work? More like Men Hanging Around Public Lavatories. Ultravox? Ultra shite. Modern Romance? Get me a gun – now. The Stranglers? Pub band. Shakin' Stevens? Welsh greaser having a fit. My God, what was left – Keith Harris and Orville? Jesus, maybe Dad was right after all – maybe Frank Sinatra *was* the answer.

I was slipping at school, which was typical of me. If my heart wasn't in it then it didn't interest me – I simply could not be arsed. And it showed – I'd been called in to see Mr Johnson, Head of Sixth Form, to talk about 'my progress'. I can remember waiting for him, outside his office. I was early, showing willing, and was idly flicking through a copy of *Smash Hits* that someone had left on the table next to the coffee machine. It was full to brimming with bollocks – a four-page feature about Boy George shopping for a frock, some nonsense about Le Bon's new boat and a piece concerning itself with the new make-up Adam Ant was endorsing – like I said; complete and utter bollocks. I skipped through the pages and something caught my eye – the flash of a raincoat, a glare of white sock, the gleam of a polished loafer – my heart skipped a broken beat; it couldn't be. Could it?

Before I had time to flick further, Mr Johnson appeared, in a whirlwind of fag ash and brandy breath. 'Come in, Lines – we have much to discuss . . .'

I stuffed the mag in my bag and followed him through to his office. He wasn't awful, in fact he was quite kind and he talked about how it wasn't uncommon for bright pupils to lose their way a little and that with the right encouragement and guidance I'd quickly be back on track. I agreed with him, told him I was well aware that I'd let myself, my family and the school down and that all of my efforts were going to be put into getting the right results the next time round. Johnson told me not to be too hard on myself and just to get my head down and enjoy my studies. I couldn't get out of there quickly enough – I needed to find out if that really was Paul in the picture.

It was. The magazine had little teaser ads dotted throughout, all featuring different images that could only be connected with Weller; the silver identity bracelet, the two-tone shoes, the back of his head. But what exactly was The Style Council? I couldn't *wait* to find out.

The Style Council seemed to me to be everything that The Jam were not. The first single, 'Speak Like A Child', certainly had a different sound – and Paul had a very different new look to match. Instead of finding it confusing like a lot of fans did, I absolutely got the whole thing straightaway – and I loved it.

'Speak Like A Child' was, to my ears at least, as fresh and vibrant and hopeful as a bright spring day. It suited the time of its release, March, and the daffodils danced in the garden to the fun new sounds spinning from my speakers. This was a welcome new world of music, and I embraced it completely – not just because it was Paul, but because I utterly dug it. The first single was a funky rush of horns and Hammond organ, backing vocals provided by unknown eighteen-year-old Tracie. I can remember now that I wasn't shocked by The Style Council, I was shocked by the fact that Paul had gone on to do something else. Perhaps it was naïve of me at the time, but I honestly didn't think that I'd see him again. I truly believed that without The Jam there would be no Paul Weller so when the Council came along I wasn't just over the moon because Paul was back, I was over the moon because he was back with something that I thoroughly loved listening to. The Style Council were . . . dramatic. I think that was one of the biggest pulls for me. I'd become dramatic through school plays and now Paul was developing his love of clothes and films and Frenchness, just like I had through *The Boy Friend*.

The Style Council also saw the introduction of the mysterious and enigmatic Cappuccino Kid, identity unknown, who provided whimsical sleeve notes for the singles. I grew to love these almost as much as the music itself. Paul's new partner in The Style Council was a certain Mick Talbot who Paul had been friends with for some time and who had played keyboards on 'The Eton Rifles' – he certainly brought something new to the party and the B-side to 'Speak Like A Child' gave big, brave clues to the new way Weller was heading. I lapped it up! The flip was called 'Party Chambers', and man, what a tune.

It was the sixties captured and bottled and put down on vinyl. I always thought it would have been just as good as an instrumental, with its crazy synths, piano and jazzy drumming – and I loved dancing to it. The video to 'Speak Like A Child' only reinforced how much Paul was enjoying his new band – I almost pissed myself laughing. Paul took the mick out of himself big style; the vid opens with PW sitting in a rocking chair on top of a hill and cuts between him and Mick larking around in a field, on an open-top London bus haring through the countryside with some hippy chicks playing the horn section like Cliff Richard in 'Summer Holiday'. They're pratting around with colourful umbrellas and leaping around like kids and the bus has 'Really Free – Aren't We?' plastered down the side. The clip's filmed in black and white and then bits of it are coloured in with what look like scratchy felt-tip pens and it is what it is, a bit of fun. Paul was sending out a message – 'I'm not as serious as you think I am.' The first time I saw it was on Saturday morning telly

– I can't remember the name of the show and I didn't know it was coming – it just jumped out at me. I dropped my sausage sarnie and phoned Rik straight away. 'Are you watching this?'

'I am, Dave. And I think he's gone mad . . . stark, staring fucking bonkers.'

The Jam didn't really do videos but, as The Style Council broadened Paul's musical output, so too did his videos. I adored the indulgent dress sense, the theatrical promo clips, his ironic view of the music business and the desperate need to disassociate himself from The Jam Army. Being in The Jam Army made you want to go to the coast and smack a rocker – but The Style Council just made me want to get my nails done. The Jam could never have made a noise like The Style Council, not even if they'd wanted to.

I was writing more and more short stories, poetry (despite never having had a thing back from Paul) and the sketches that I was collaborating on with Lizzie were getting really good. I was growing into the direction I wanted to go in despite being in a school which frowned on anything out of the ordinary. Paul was developing his new path and The Style Council encouraged me to find mine. It was the only support

I got. Dad didn't know what to make of my dreams and I think Mum found my work embarrassing to read – as for Chris and Phil, I think they just thought their big brother was more like a big ponce. I can remember the first time I saw The Style Council play live on the box. Peter Powell introduced them on BBC Two and Paul was wearing mascara and eyeliner with a pastel-yellow jersey draped around his shoulders. Mum took one look and said, 'Ooh – he's gone all weird . . .'

I vividly remember one night which helped push me forward when things at school had turned into a real grind. The studying for resits now held about as much interest for me as a jam jar full of warm wank and all I wanted to do was write, write and write again. All I could see before me was a huge, great wall. I'd sort of started seeing Hazel Rimmer, who I'd met through the musical and who'd left school and gone to work in a bank. It was a Saturday night in the Bird in Hand, which was like an extension to school at the weekends. Hazel was the same age as me and looked alarmingly grown-up. She had a lady's handbag, blonde hair in a bob that looked like it knew when you were overdrawn and an agreeable habit of wearing her blouse a size too small with too many buttons undone. Curiously, she had a pretty but very, very small face. I always thought it was like French kissing a cat.

It was half-seven and the Bird in Hand was filling up quickly as I elbowed my way through the crowd to the long bar. I bought drinks for me and Hazel, with her money. She earned a decent wage and always paid for my cigarettes and our drinks and we'd been seeing each other for about eight weeks. I liked her, but she was very bossy and assertive and she was a massive Haircut One Hundred fan, which was the biggest drawback because she was constantly trying to get me to tuck my ski jumper into my jeans like bloody Nick Heyward. As you know, I absolutely *loathed* Haircut One Hundred. I thought that they looked like catalogue models.

'There you are, Haze. Half a lager and black.' I picked the glass up off the tray and handed it to her.

She looked worried. 'Um, thanks. And just who are all the other drinks for?'

'Us. It's a scrum up there. We don't want to spend all night waiting to get served, do we?'

'No, you're right. Good thinking. Was there any change from that tenner?'

'Not really . . .'

Hazel sipped her drink and lit a John Player Special. I hated them, they were far too strong for me. I lit a Silk Cut and steadily worked my way through three Pernod and blacks, a pint of lager, half a cider and a rum and Coke. Hazel managed to make her drink last all through mine and launched into a fascinating conversation about variable base rates. I don't know if it was just the drink but I felt very sleepy. Hazel told me about the people she worked with and the people she caught the bus to work with and how she'd get a staff rate on the loan she was going to take out to buy a Mini Metro. Just as my head felt as if it was about to drop off, Lizzie Marlow came into view, through the tap room and into the main bar. She saw me and started jumping up and down, waving rolled up scripts at me and she pointed at her watch and then at me, mouthing 'In a minute'. I waved back and Hazel went to the loo and to get more drinks in. I watched her totter off, in her deep cherry-red miniskirt and her white high heels and I was picturing her without any clothes on when Lizzie sidled up next to me. 'There you are, brush-head; our first scripts typed up ready for rehearsal!'

'Thanks – well done, you.'

'Don't mention it.'

Lizzie rubbed my new haircut. It was cropped way short, like a crew cut that had just grown out, like Paul's new look but with shorter sideburns. People kept coming up, scratching and rubbing it. I didn't mind, it reminded me of a woman on the telly the previous night talking about how when she was pregnant everyone felt as if they had the right to stroke her swollen belly. It was the same with spiky hair – it was an open invitation for people to mess it up. Lizzie was dressed in denim dungarees – she looked as if she should be presenting *Play Away*.

'So, tell me how it's all going with *Hazel*?' She cocked her head on one side and beamed at me like a lunatic, like Animal, the drummer from *The Muppets*.

'Why did you say her name like that?'

'Like what?'

'Like the way you just did? Like *that*.'

'Easy, tiger. It's just . . .'

'It's just what?'

'It's just that you and Hazel don't seem, you know, you don't seem suited for each other.' Lizzie patted her pockets for her fags, couldn't find them, so took one of Hazel's.

'And what, is that a bad thing?'

'You're just a very unlikely couple.'

'So what's the fucking problem?' I snapped this back at her with some real venom and she looked shocked. Sod it, it was the drink, I didn't mean to be rude.

'Fuck, David. I'm sorry – right? I didn't mean to upset you, I didn't *mean* anything. I was just saying, that's all. I'm going. Ring me about rehearsals.' She got up, ruffled my hair again and gave me a peck on the cheek. I was glad, it showed me we were still friends. I was an idiot sometimes, I really was. Hazel came back with the drinks and I finished mine in one. 'Come on, I'll walk you home,' I said.

Hazel was not happy and neither was I. We walked for five minutes; her house wasn't far from the pub. She lived close to Kate and I asked if she knew her well. It was the first we'd spoken since we left the Bird. I didn't even hear her reply because of the blood gushing around my head as I fell over, face down into her father's semicircular flower bed. It wasn't even nine at night and I could see two Hazels, two open front doors and two Mr Rimmers looking mightily pissed off. I lay sprawled across his front garden and the scripts lay scattered around me. Both Hazels helped me up, gathered the scripts and stuffed them into my hand.

They leaned in close, I thought she was going to kiss me but she didn't, she just whispered in my ear, 'Don't ever fucking phone me again – it's over.' I didn't know how to react. I didn't know what was worse; the fact that I'd just been dumped or that as she leaned in, the breath from her warm mouth and the heat off her tongue travelled down through my ear and straight to my balls. What kind of man was I who got turned on even when he's being dumped?

It was an early summer breeze which blew me slightly sober. There was a dampness in the air and I stumbled through the streets, not knowing where I was going. Another pub for another drink? Back home to bed? No, I ended up just walking past the big, red-brick houses with their big cars spilling out of their big drives onto the streets. Jesus, even the wing mirrors on the BMWs had their own hanging baskets. I wanted to read the scripts so I sat on someone's front wall and looked at them underneath the lamplight. I sparked up a cigarette and whistled smoke from my lips, watching it cloud the night's sky. It blurred out the stars in front of my eyes and I started to shiver. I was cold and my teeth chattered and I was suddenly washed away by a tide of depression. I'd been dumped, I'd upset Lizzie,

I hated school, and I felt lost. It was down to the drink, but a stupid idea came into my head – I decided to set fire to the scripts to keep warm. After all, what was that ridiculous idea wanting to write? I took out my Bic lighter and flicked the flame free, drawing it to the edge of the first page. 'Is that you, David Lines?' There was a voice behind me, out of the night, and now I knew where I was. I recognised the voice with its soft tone of the Tyne and its tenderness warmed me from six feet away. It's a lovely feeling when a voice smiles at you. 'Yeah, it's me, Mr Blyton.'

Kate's dad looked genuinely appalled at the sight of me, covered in mud, stinking of booze, shoes caked with soil. He screwed up his nose and peered out at me from behind his steamy spectacles. His hair was made even whiter by the slight sheen of the rain and he looked like he might want to give me a lecture, but he didn't, instead he just knocked his pipe out on the back of his hand and said, 'I was thinking about having a wee Scotch – care to come inside and join me?'

'Thanks. I'd like that.' I spluttered the words out in a half sob, they tripped over themselves and I disguised the fact that I felt like crying by adding, 'A very kind offer.'

'Good. I've been meaning to ask Kate how your

writing was coming along. Right, then – let's get inside where it's warm.'

I moved to follow him and he pointed at my scripts on the pavement, the rain splodging the words, merging them into one wet, inky mess. 'What's that? Looks important . . .' I picked them up and we ran out of the rain.

The kitchen smelled of chicken soup and freshly ground coffee. There was a photograph of Kate held against the fridge door by a magnetic letter K. It had been taken on a beach with mile after mile of golden sands stretching out behind her and I wondered where it was taken. She was much younger in the picture, in her very early teens, I guess, and the sun had brought out her freckles. Kate was waving a Cadbury's 99 flake the way Groucho Marks did with his cigar. She looked happy.

'How about some coffee with a wee nip inside? That should warm us up.'

'Lovely.' I didn't know what to say next, so I just sat there. And grinned. I liked being in Kate's kitchen, I could feel her here as well as see her on the fridge. I smiled back at her.

'Tell me, how's your Big Dream coming along?' He

poured the coffee, didn't put any milk in, but unscrewed the top of his bottle of Scotch and slopped in a nice, syrupy-coloured slug. I could smell it and it smelled good. It reminded me of Grampa Lines.

'My Big Dream's turning into a fucking nightmare, to tell the truth, Mr Blyton. Oh, sorry.'

He took a mouthful of his drink and started packing Condor Ready Rubbed tobacco into his pipe.

'Call me Jim. In what way is it turning into a fucking nightmare?'

'God, I don't know, I just feel really . . . lost. Do you mind if I have a cigarette?'

He laughed, and his eyes danced and sparkled from the light of his match, just the same way Kate's had with the fairy lights reflected in them.

'Do I mind? Look, when this old briar gets going we'll need to open windows. Go ahead and smoke your cigarette with pleasure, but tell me why it's a nightmare and why you feel lost.'

I lit up and with the cigarette, the bitter coffee and the Scotch nicely burning my throat, I lit up a bit inside myself as well. 'I don't know why I feel lost. I just can't seem to stay focused on anything. It's all gone a bit . . . wobbly.'

Jim patted the tobacco down inside the bowl, put the match to it and sucked, drawing the flame in like a willow bending in the wind. He smiled sweetly at his briar and nodded at me to go on.

'Oh, I suppose it's because I should be doing my A levels now and I'm not. I'm having to do these bloody resits and the plan's gone wrong. I'm not on target, I'm not motivated and I'm basically all at sea. I suppose the truth is that I'm distracted by what I want to be . . .'

'Hmm. So what's this?' He pointed his pipe at my papers, prodded at my scripts.

'It's for the sixth-form review. I wrote some sketches with Lizzie Marlow.'

'Can I have a look?'

'Sure, if you can read them. They're a bit wet. Sorry.'

'It's not me you should be apologising to. It's Lizzie. Show some respect for your work or it'll go nowhere. Shuffle them over, then.'

I passed him over the wet, sorry pieces of paper and he read them for a few minutes, a smile here, a titter there and then he burst out laughing. Someone was laughing at what I'd written – what an amazing feeling.

'This sketch here is hilarious! The one about a man

who takes his right hand out for dinner because he feels guilty about wanking so much, he wants to give himself something back!'

'I know. It was the cheapest date he'd ever had – and however badly the evening went he'd still be certain to pull.'

We howled like dogs, and from behind Jim's shoulder I could see Kate, laughing back from behind her freckles on the fridge and it was then, right then, that it hit me straight between the eyes. I made a pledge with Kate, a promise to be kept forever, and what's worse is that I made it right there, at that very kitchen table. How could I dream of giving up? How dare I doubt myself?

Jim stopped laughing, extended his long, thin arm and pointed his pipe at me. 'You've got to stay on your path. You've got to keep to it and you absolutely must not stray off it, not for a moment. That's what my Kate's doing – she's on her way now, and you could be as well – just don't you dare take your eye off the ball. You do that and you're done for. This is funny stuff you've written. How about I drive you home and you get a good night's sleep and then work on some more. If it's in you, if the talent's there, then all you have to do is to tease it out. But you're not going to do that getting pissed every night, understand?'

I was about to ask him just what the hell he knew about it all, but then, as he topped up his mug with Scotch, I thought that perhaps he'd been there, seen it and that maybe it wasn't that far behind him. I wondered if he'd had the same conversation with Kate?

'Point taken. How's Kate doing at college?'

His face beamed a smile as wide as the Tyne. 'My little girl's doing just fine, thanks.'

'That's good to know. Tell her I said hello?'

'I will. Now, let's get you home to bed. And don't forget what I said – it's the way the world works . . .'

We drove back to my house, I got out of the car and got straight into bed. I was asleep before my head hit the pillow.

12

A Paris

A Paris was the first EP released by The Style Council, and it was unleashed into an unknowing world on a balmy summer day: 18 August, 1983. Since the first single, 'Speak Like A Child', they'd also released 'Money-Go-Round', a highly political rap oozing with funk and spunk, guile and bile. It only went to prove Paul's point about his lack of respect for the music industry – it was a deeply uncommercial sound, a breathy attack on a country gripped by Tory rule, featuring a taunting, sarcastic trombone played by Annie Whitehead. Orange Juice's Zeke Manyika played drums on it. Paul donated his royalties to Youth CND and, despite it not being tailor-made for the charts, it gained a great feat in peaking at number eleven. 'Money-Go-Round' (which took its title from an old Kinks song) also featured backing vocals by DC Lee – ex-Wham! backing vocalist. She didn't know it then, but DC was going to play a big part in the rest of Paul's life – both on the record, and off.

It was a day devoid of cloud, in late August, and in the early autumnal mists, the greyness of my winter days settling in at the sixth form seemed but a distant memory away. I was in the back garden, wearing a beret and busy tucking into a plateful of snails.

The Style Council's music and muse had shifted in a distinctly European direction of late, and in particular Paul had looked to all things French for inspiration. Both his music and his clothes were culled from Parisian bars, clubs and cafés and – quite literally – I'd followed suit. *A Paris* had been released two weeks earlier and I simply could not believe my ears – I'd died and gone to heaven. Paul had adopted the fantastic French style of the Sorbonne which I had so fallen in love with during *The Boy Friend* and there it was right on the record sleeve – Paul and Mick posing for the camera looking incredibly cool, wearing the most stylish outfits topped-off with colourful cashmere sweaters tossed casually round their shoulders in the shadow of the glorious Eiffel Tower.

Likewise, I'd thrown a sweater around my shoulders and myself headlong into full-frontal Frenchness. As soon as I'd seen what Paul was doing with this look I immediately switched my brand of cigarette from Silk Cut to Gitanes and, consequently, spent the next six months peeling bits of tobacco – and skin – from my bottom lip. I was sporting a very high maintenance short French crop and had started cycling to the baker's early each morning for freshly baked croissants or continental pastries.

'Now then, lad – what can I be gettin' ya?'

'*Deux pains au chocolat, s'il vous plait*.'

'Maureen! Come quick – it's that simple lad – he's back again!'

My new obsession was rapidly taking over my life. 'Mum – where's Dad? I haven't seen him for ages.'

'Try the greenhouse – it's your best bet.'

'What on earth's he been doing down there for the past four days?'

'It's probably you and your sodding garlic with everything. You've literally driven the poor man out of the house with the stench . . .'

Mum uncorked a bottle of white wine and poured herself a glass. It went down in one gulp. I reached for the bottle and poured myself one as well. 'Ridiculous behaviour. I mean, moving into the greenhouse just because of a few herbs. Some people will never realise the true value of cross-cultural pollination . . .'

Mum poured herself another glass and this one went down as quickly as the last. 'Your tea'll be ready in five minutes.'

'Lovely. What I really feel like this evening is something vaguely Provençal, something nice and light – maybe a sardine and anchovy salad?'

'It's Findus crispy pancakes and oven chips. Tell your father I'll bring them down to him before *Nationwide* starts, there's a good boy . . .'

I loved *A Paris* so much. Even though it only contained four tracks, I listened to it endlessly, hour after hour. The numbers were all stunning, yet as different from each other as could be – it was as if they were from the four corners of the universe and The Council had drawn them together and released them as one. Again, the hilarious sleeve notes were provided by the shadowy figure that is the Cappuccino Kid and here they revealed that these recordings were made in Paris between the 12–17 of June and that they were recorded there because they felt that they all had a similar 'blue mood' and a certain French flavour about them. That's an understatement: this record was so French it had to have been pressed through a garlic crusher. The songs are: 'The Paris Match', which, according to the Cappuccino Kid, he originally wrote for leading French chanteuse Suzanne Toblat, who recorded it with a French lyric but it was yet to see a release. (Could that possibly be Mick's sister, then?); 'Party Chambers', which I've already talked about, albeit with a special arrangement from Suzanne's fictitious brother; 'Le Depart' – which I'll come to with arse cheeks suitably clenched with embarrassment in a bit; and finally there's 'Long Hot Summer', the current single. This was perfect for oozing out of portable trannies on beaches and, on that particular day, its lovely, sexy, hypnotic chords wafted out of the French windows of our dining room, over the patio and mingled with the sticky, buttery garlic I'd just fried my snails in.

I had unearthed the six sorry snails by searching for them in the gap between the potting shed and next-door's fence. It was foul down there, wet and dark, the dank environment providing me with more should I get a taste for the slimy, crunchy critters. I plucked the snails out of their shells with the late Grampa Lines's pickle fork that only used to come out at Christmas. Then I fried the fuckers in a small saucepan, along with some Anchor butter and two cloves of garlic. Before then, garlic didn't exist in our house – I had to go to the grocer's near Kate's to get my grubby little mitts on those alien bulbs.

I sat outside at the table on the patio with a glass of white wine to wash down the snails. Mum, Dad, Chris and Phil were inside the house having cheese on toast and watching me, pointing and laughing like insane people. I popped a grey, leathery coil into my mouth and crunched down on it, trying to ignore the warm, wet juice as it burst into my mouth and oozed down my gagging throat. Then, just in time and with as much – or as little – dignity as I could muster, I quickly took off my black felt beret and used it to catch my own hot vomit. Chris was laughing so much that he fired molten Cracker Barrel out of both nostrils.

After I'd recovered from my unholy tea I cycled round to Rik's to watch the video for 'Long Hot

Summer' for the first time. Rik was just back from a week in Cap Ferret where his parents had a timeshare in a static caravan. We switched on the television. When Paul and Mick appeared there was a silence in the air, a terrible, violent silence. Rik dropped his Ovaltine in his lap. Time stood still around us and my jaw dropped, a bacon sandwich suspended midway between my hand and mouth. Our eyes were wide open, our hair stood on end and it felt as if we were frozen forever to the brown, Dralon sofa. I've just watched it again – and I can see why.

The video opens with Mick and Paul punting around on the Cam like a couple of prime fairies. Weller's stretched out on this punt, open-shirted, wearing sawn-off denim shorts and is happily touching himself up, his fingers fluttering over his chest and stomach, pausing at the top of his shorts. Mick's in white flannels and a blazer, and is gaily biting at the willow which weeps from the bank of the river down into the water as he steers Paul through it. Throughout the video, an unknown Frenchman playing bongos pops up and waves at the two boys, then disappears off somewhere to let them carry on enjoying themselves. Then, they moor up, throw down a gingham picnic rug and dance around in the summer sun. Paul's now got his top off, the curious Frenchie's hard at it on his bongos and now Weller and Mick are laying head to head on the rug, fondling each other's ears, giggling, licking their lips and generally at it like a couple of rampant homosexuals. *This* is the ex-lead singer of The Jam?

After what seemed like a lifetime Rik finally broke the silence. 'Dave, what does it all mean?'

I knew exactly what it meant – and I loved it. What it meant, was that Paul was getting himself further and further away from The Jam Army. This thing he'd created, The Style Council, felt to me like theatre. If The Jam's had been a pint of mild, The Style Council stuck an umbrella and a cherry in it and they didn't have an army, they had a flower arranging class who met once a week in the village hall. 'It's a joke, Rik. That's all – he's just enjoying himself, being free of The Jam. They're being, you know, ironic.'

'Well, I wish he wouldn't be quite so queer about it.' And then he stood up and took his trousers off. I have to admit to being a bit worried but then I spotted what looked like third-degree burns on his knob area from the Ovaltine spillage. 'Do you think they're going out with each other, Dave? Do you think he's gone over to the other side?'

'What, like boyfriend and . . . boyfriend?'

'Yeah. Exactly. Do you think him and Talbot are at it with each other?'

'I sincerely doubt it. They're just having a giggle, Rik.'

'Hmm . . . well I'm not laughing.'

'I can't imagine Bruce and Rick having a threesome with Paul, can you? I mean, who'd be doing what to whom?'

'Linesy, stop it. You're saying things which'd get you burnt at the stake a hundred years ago.' Rik disappeared into another room and came back wearing an alarming pair of his sister's hot pants. 'Dave?'

'What?'

'Do you think they bum each other?'

This was getting out of hand. 'No, Richard, I most certainly do not. And anyway, who cares if they do? It's a bit of fun, chance for a bit of publicity.'

'Doesn't look like fun to me. It looks like he's been having a go on Mick's blue-veined flute.'

'Enough now. Let's watch it again. I'm sure it's not as bad as you imagine.'

Rik rewound the tape and we checked it out again. It was just as we saw it the first time. We weren't dreaming and Rik was not at all convinced. I could see his point, the ex-front man of Britain's biggest power-pop trio of all time openly having sex with some bloke who looked like our milkman. But I thought it was inspired! Weller was destroying everything and starting again from scratch. What magnificent balls he must have had.

Rik asked me if I fancied another coffee and a frame or two of snooker. I said yes to the coffee but no to the snooks on the grounds of me having to stand up. If I did, there'd be absolutely no way of disguising my raging hard-on. I sipped my Mellow Birds and concentrated all my thoughts on Alison Moyet till my prick finally calmed down.

Wearing a beret, cooking snails and eating croissants just wasn't enough for me. I needed to take my Frenchness one stage further. I always have done, you know, wanted to take everything one stage further, go that little bit extra. I never know when to stop, and back then, especially back then, I always ended up looking like a monumental unit. I was allowed, though. I was, after all, that most self-aware yet unaware of creatures – I was a teenager.

No, I wasn't content just with the records and the style and the sleeve notes and the ever changing haircuts – I'd decided to do something much more drastic. I decided to change my name. By simply placing a stylish accent over the letter 'e' in Lines, I could transform myself overnight from plain old David Lines to *DJ Linés* – pronounced Lin-ay. What a master stroke! I asked Dad what he thought before going to see my form tutor, Miss Rose. I wanted her to circulate the news throughout the school that I'd changed my name, and I'd made an appointment to see her the following day. I thought I'd just run it by Mum and Dad first, just to see what they thought.

We were out in the garden, early evening. Dad was in his deck chair studying the 'Spot the Ball' competition in the *Evening Post*. We'd both got cups of coffee and were having a nice cigarette each after tea. Mum was washing up and Phil and Chris were inside watching *Blockbusters.* A blackbird chirruped from the fence and Dad passed me the paper. 'What do you think? I reckon the ball's about an inch above the crossbar, just next to that weirdo's head.'

'What, the guy who looks like Howard Jones?'

'Who's Howard Jones?'

'He's a tit with terrible hair. And a bald mate who dances around like a cretin.'

'Sounds about right. I'm sticking a cross right smack bang in the centre of Howard Jones's forehead, lad.'

'Good choice. Dad?'

'What?'

'What do you know about our background?'

'Right now, it's an overgrown hollyhock in front of a peeling garden fence which your mother keeps nagging me to sand down and paint.'

'No, I mean, like, what do you know about our family heritage?'

Dad coughed as he drew on his cigarette and clutched his chest. His eyes rolled back in astonishment and he just about managed to splutter out, 'What are you on about?'

'I just thought that there might be some hidden heritage to our surname. It's something we were talking about at school, you know, like where our names might come from and someone said that Lines was probably foreign and, quite possibly, French.'

Dad sucked on his cigarette with such tremendous force I feared that he might actually swallow the damn thing. He crinkled his eyes and cleared his throat and he shook his head slowly. 'You do come out with some shit, son.'

'What?'

'French? If I didn't know you as well as I do, it'd be laughable. But it isn't, lad, it's just sad.' He flicked his fag end into the forsythia and seconds later it sent little smoke signals back.

'I don't know what you mean, Dad. I was just wondering if we could be from France originally and that we might have been the Linés from Lyon.'

He lit another cigarette and it burned and blazed almost in anger and with one almighty suck the thin, white cylinder was reduced by almost half. 'The Linés from Lyon?'

Smoke tornadoed out of his nose and there was so much of it Dad's head was instantly replaced by a grey, fluffy cloud. Through the fog came his voice. 'Have you ever wondered what it is that makes you so unhappy being yourself? All you do is want not to be you. That's it, from the minute you wake up to the minute you go to bed you spend all day thinking about being someone else. In fact I wouldn't be at all surprised if you dreamt of being someone else. If it's not that wanker Weller then it's some doddery love-struck pensioner in that ruddy awful play. And now you want to be French. What's wrong with you, lad?'

'Nothing, Dad. I just –'

'Don't nothing me. Have you any idea how it makes me and your mum feel?'

'Dad, I'm sorry, I really am but I don't know what you mean. Please don't be cross with me.'

His milky grey eyes emerged out of the fug and they showed not that he was cross, but something much, much worse. They pitied me. 'Your grandfather, my father, he was an orphan. Rejected as a tiny wee baby and left with strangers and he went on to become something, to be someone, to build a business, to protect others in need during the war and to find a wife. He made me, and me and your mother made you and your brothers and we try, me and your mum, to give you everything that we can. We moved here, to Leeds, to give you a better life, a better start and what do you do? You become obsessed with some stupid bloody group, you dress like them, cut your hair like them and now you want to turn your back not only on us, but on Grampa Lines as well. Is this family such a bloody pain to you that you constantly want to be someone else?'

I said nothing and Dad got up and went inside. I was stunned – it felt as if he hadn't said that much to me in years.

13

Le Depart

Kate came home from college. She was back from Bretton Hall for the weekend; I knew that she was home because Suzanne Tappin, Kate's friend, told me. We had walked back from sixth form together the previous Wednesday and she slyly dropped it into conversation on the way. 'Are you going to the Bird on Saturday?'

'Dunno. Why?'

'Oh, Kate's back, that's all – just thought you might like to know . . .'

It was Saturday morning and the house was empty

– everyone else was at the supermarket. Since that day in the garden, with Dad, I'd got the impression that maybe he was speaking not just for himself, but for Mum, Chris and Phil too and it sat uneasily with me. I wasn't purposefully being a pain – it was just something which seemed to come naturally.

I called Kate – it was my ideal and opportune moment. I sat on the stairs on the second to bottom step and sipped my piping hot cup of freshly ground coffee and sucked on my Gitanes as the telephone rang and rang and rang . . . Before me lay the letterbox and, as the postman's sinister silhouette approached the glass door and the post plopped through it, not for one moment did I bother to look up. I'd given up sending my poetry to Paul the day that The Jam died.

The phone rang for what seemed like an age, and then she answered, her voice sounded warm and snuggly, like she had just woken up.

'Hello, Kate – it's David.'

'Huh? David who?'

'It's me – David. David Lines.'

'Oh. Oh, hi.'

'Yeah . . . hi.' I could hear her exhaling her Silk Cut. Actually, I could *picture* her exhaling her Silk Cut.

'Sorry, David – was there something? It's lovely to hear from you and all that, but I've got a bath running.'

'Oh, God, sorry – look, I know you're just going to be running around like mad and everything and probably seeing hundreds of people this weekend, but I was just ringing to see if you'd like to meet up for a drink or something.'

'Darling, that would be utterly lovely, but I'm afraid my time's not mine for a moment this weekend, not for a second is it mine. On top of seeing absolutely everyone, I've got a piano lesson, I have to have tea with my aunt, I've got an essay to write and I've got to get my hair done. Sorry, sweetheart – maybe next time.'

'I didn't know that you played piano.' Jesus Christ – was there no end to this woman's talents?

'I don't, not properly, I'm just sort of learning. Playing the piano has always been an ambition of mine – I think it's just the most amazing thing to be able to do. When I see a man play the piano, play his big, broad fingers over those black and white keys it sends a shiver down my shoulders, right down my spine and in-between my legs. Seriously, sugar – it's better than sex, you know?'

Dear God in heaven. 'Yeah, Kate – I know just what you mean. That's exactly the reason why I took it up – it feels the same for me – exactly the same.'

Wait a minute, you ponce, what are you on about?

I heard her catch her breath three estates and two miles away. She was impressed. 'I had no idea. Well, well, David – you *are* a dark horse. Are you terribly good at it?'

I had never been near one of the things before. 'Now you come to mention it, I've just got my grade eight.'

I could feel the electricity coming down the phone. The hairs on my neck stood up like a Christmas jumper rubbed by a New Year's party balloon.

'Oh, you clever, clever man.'

That was music to my ears. 'Actually, I've been working on a title composition of my own. In fact, that's one of the reasons I was calling you – I wanted to let you know it's almost finished . . . and it's about you, Kate.'

What was I *saying*? Yet again I took it spectacularly beyond what I needed to. Prat!

Deadly silence, then, 'David, I'm flattered. You *are* talented.'

Exactly what was I talented in? Digging holes so deep I needed the fire brigade to help me out of them?

'Nonsense – it's nothing really.'

'Nothing? Rubbish. You sweet, sweet thing. I demand to hear it as soon as possible.'

Oh, no. Oh, bollocks – I'd really gone and done it, Linesy, you cretin. It was going way too fast – and it was time to bail out.

'Well, maybe one day. The piece is all about how I feel every time that I see you and then how painful it is when we part. The first section deals with how happy I am when I see you and the second addresses how sad I am when you leave.'

More silence, then, 'Oh, look what you've gone and done – you've only made me go and cry.'

'Please don't cry, Kate. Save your tears till you've heard it – it's far from brilliant.'

Dickhead. She'll want to hear it. Why didn't I think, man?

'Then I demand to hear this composition. I demand to hear it right away and I've just had the most delicious of ideas, my angel!'

Oh, Christ. 'What?'

'Come round to the house tonight. Mum and Dad are going out to play bridge and we can have the place to ourselves. You can give me my own private recital; how thrilling! Who knows what might happen . . .'

Prat. Arse. Wanker. Loon. Idiot. Moron. Spacker. Spaz. Tosser. Fuckwit. Spunkhead. When, oh, when, would I ever learn? Christ, cue Batsignal – I didn't know one end of a piano from the other – what was I gonna do? Wait a minute – what was that above my head? It was only a bloody great light bulb . . .

'That's a very tempting offer, Kate, but to spare my blushes – I'm a very nervous performer – would you mind if I played it to you down the phone?'

I could feel the warmth of her breath as she sighed, 'God, how romantic – please do . . .' I took the phone into the living room and was into the records like a flash. Out came the *A Paris* EP and on went 'Le Depart'. I switched to the phone in the lounge and began the charade.

The vinyl was out of the sleeve and straight onto the turntable in one second flat. I cued up the track and down went the needle. 'Kate, just give me a moment to compose myself.' I turned down the volume and dropped the needle into the play-in groove. My hand shook so much it took all my concentration not to scratch the thing to buggery. Jesus, I had to stay calm. The horror of her having maybe heard it somewhere before, on the radio or at a friend's place only added to the terror with which I watched the needle ride the groove. The possibility of me appearing to be a class A idiot was all too real. I froze with fear. The needle was almost there. I turned the volume back up and then positioned the phone midway between the two speakers at a distance of about five feet. I took a deep breath.

The haunting, melancholic opening bars of The Style Council's moody, grieving piano piece slid off the record, out of the Wharfedales and down the phone line to the girl of my dreams. The music conjured up images of such loss, of such remorse and regret, of Paris streets soaked in rain, of too many cigarettes and too many tears, of wandering aimlessly from café to bar, wondering when I'd see her once more, of empty nights spent trying to forget. The crashing, dashing crescendo went as quickly as it came, with its final, plodding notes echoing away like footsteps in the distance.

I just about managed to get the volume back down before the needle ran headlong into the run-out groove and the static from the almighty, horrific collision gave the game away. I waited a heartbeat and put the phone up to my ear. I could hear Kate fighting back the tears.

Dear God, what had I gone and done? 'Hello? Kate?'

The ignition sound of a lighter and I could almost

taste the blue plume as she exhaled.

'David, my love, that was beautiful. A work of pure, shimmering beauty. Thank you so much.'

I hated it, I was a fraud and I deserved to be flogged for making her cry. 'Thanks, but really, it was nothing.' I was virtually crushed under the crippling weight that was my own false modesty.

'And you wrote that – for me?'

'I did, Kate, I wrote it just for you . . .'

'I was lost for words. Tell me, what's it called?'

'Um, it's called "Departure". And I'm just glad that you liked it.'

'Like it? I adore it! You really are the most brilliant boy. I'm so touched.'

That was my chance. At the moment when I was about to confess my undying love for her, Mum burst through the front door, dumped down two bags of shopping and screamed at the top of her voice, 'Thank God you've turned that bloody depressing drivel off! It makes me want to kill myself! People can hear it in the street you had it turned up so loud – and they're happily throwing themselves in front of cars!'

I couldn't get my hand over the mouthpiece quickly enough.

14

Shout To The Top!

School was getting me nowhere fast. It was no good for me at all; education was making me physically sick. I was tired and bored beyond belief with my studies and I'd just sit and stare for hour after hour at pages of textbooks, my revision notes and study timetables; all amounted to nothing. It was depressing me. I had to get out of school for good – I had to get out for the good of my health.

Then The Style Council released 'Shout To The Top!', and the first time I heard it I knew what I had to do. This song so reminded me of The Jam's passion and bite, it inspired me to do something about my situation. It made me get up off my backside and take control of my destiny. It may have taken me a while to get to this point, but when Paul Weller split The Jam he taught me one massive lesson: he taught me to never be afraid of walking away from something you're not happy with. The fury and anger seeped through this single. Paul had taken an uplifting melody, dripped strings all over it and married together the catchiest tune with the bitterest of lyrics. It came out of the ring punching and dancing and forceful and it drove me to make my mind up; I was going to walk out of school as quickly as I could. I hated Paul Weller's guts when he walked out of The Jam, but once I'd come to my decision I couldn't thank him enough. I'd seen how being free of it had helped him blossom as a writer and stretch him as a musician and that he'd moved on to something more, something fresh and exciting – which was just what I needed.

If I was one day going to stay true to my dream and try and be a writer, then I needed to surround myself with books. Once I'd decided that, the answer was clear – I would try and get a job in a bookshop. The next step was to tell Mum and Dad . . .

I think, looking back, that it was more of a disappointment than they let on at the time. Dad was less happy than Mum, and at first I think he felt that I'd let him down again, this time by not seeing something through to the end. Dad had left school without anything to write home about and it was only natural he wanted me to take myself further than he had. Our conversations always took place outside, and now, writing about them, I can see why: it was because if we had them inside we had nowhere to run to when they got heated.

We were sitting next to the rockery, drinking tea on a Tuesday evening. Dad had been to see the doctor about a cough and cold he couldn't seem to shift and so was home earlier than normal. He looked drained, washed out. It wasn't the best time to talk to him about leaving school, but I wanted to make my peace and not justify myself to him. 'Dad, I'm only doing this because I want to try and make something of my life and not just fester away at school. I want to get out there and have a go at life, you know?' He looked at the sky and then at his shoes and then he looked at me. His pale eyes creased and he scratched his chin. It had a heavy shadow on it, his eyes had bags under them and he seemed saddened by the thought of me turning in my studies.

'And you do this by leaving school to work in a shop?'

'Not just any shop, Dad, a *bookshop*.'

'A shop is a shop is a shop, believe me, lad, I know. It doesn't matter whether you're selling Shakespeare or a short back and sides – what you're doing is just that: shop work.'

'I can't believe you just said that.'

'Why ever not? It's perfectly true.'

'Think about it, Dad. Grampa Lines was the best barber in Bridgford, if not the entire Midlands, and you were the second best. By calling it just shop work you're saying that what Grampa Lines did amounted to no more than what some kid does as a Saturday job on a till in Tesco's, right?'

My father hung his head and searched his pockets for a fag. He hadn't any on him. 'Have one of mine,' I said, and he took it and stared at it and for a moment I thought he was going to cry.

'Look, Davey, you're eighteen years old – you've got a long time to decide what you're going to do with your life. Just don't rush anything, that's all I ask.'

'Dad, I'm seventeen.'

'Are you really? It all seems much longer than that . . .' And he passed me back my cigarette and walked slowly inside. I smoked mine and sat and thought and the more I thought about it, the more I was convinced I was doing the right thing. Mum stood on the step up to the back door and gave me a little wave. I waved back and she came and sat next to me.

I loved my dad and I hoped and I prayed that he knew it. I'd decided to prove myself to him by making it all by myself in the outside world. I told her this and she snuggled up next to me and took hold of my hand. 'Your father loves you very, very much and don't you ever think otherwise. We all do, we all love you, it's just that you always seem to go overboard. You don't just want to leave school, you want to be a writer. It's not normal behaviour, don't get me wrong, I happen to think that starting off in a bookshop's a very sensible place to begin, but your father, he wanted more for you than working in a shop. You can see that, can't you, love?' She squeezed my hand and I squeezed hers back.

'I do see that, of course I do, but I wish that Dad would see the bigger picture, see that me wanting to work in a bookshop'll lead to bigger and better things.'

Mum stood up. 'Right, then – it looks like we need to find you a job . . .'

The *Yorkshire Post*'s recruitment section comes out every Thursday. For five weeks on the trot we all pored over the different positions and then, under the heading marked 'General Vacancies', we found one which might as well have read 'David Lines – Apply for this Position – Now!' It was Chris who spotted it first – a position at Austick's University Bookshop, in Leeds, with good rates of pay and the chance of becoming a trainee buyer. I showed it to Mum and Dad and they told me to go for it.

With The Style Council, Paul had begun to show his lighter side, constantly taking the piss out of himself, presenting an air of irony hitherto unseen. But the music press didn't get it; the *NME* didn't do irony, they probably thought it was like coppery. When Weller took the piss out of himself, by prancing through summer poppy fields holding hands with Mick, colluding with the Cappuccino Kid on flowery sleeve notes, coming out with statements like 'I think that French boys are the most beautiful in the world', showing his feminine side and posing for pictures, not in front of the Union Flag, but with France's tricolour as a backdrop, he got up the wrong people's noses. Some magazine said 'Weller's not a visionary – he's a hod carrier.' Whatever, with Paul as my guide and mentor I'd taken to becoming more pretentious than ever: cigarette holder, slicked-back hair, cravat, the works. And at my interview, I excelled at being a fop and a ponce like my life depended on it.

Ten days later, after I'd been invited to interview, I sat on the top deck of a bus, the 164 from Garforth to Leeds. My appointment was three hours away and my journey would take thirty minutes at most. I looked out of the upstairs window and took in the graveyard below, the breaker's yard, the dairy yard and the tank factory. There were washing lines in Colton and they stretched from one side of the street to the other. I closed my eyes tight shut, and as I did, I pictured myself riding the bus, up above the clouds, looking down on the rows and rows of houses, soaring over the rooftops and sailing away to a promised land littered with literature and peppered with sparkling, colourful conversation. I was heady at the idea, excited by the thought that this great, shining chance could bring me a new and challenging life. Just for a moment I had to steady myself against the back of the seat in front of mine on which someone had scrawled, in bright green marker pen, 'Shaz Fucks Kev and Gaz'.

In Leeds with time to kill, I embraced The Style Council's love of café society and took time to prepare myself, to get into character for the interview in a coffee house in the Merrion Centre. The Andromeda was a fabulous place. All life was there; behind the counter a fat Greek operated a Gaggia machine, just like the one on the sleeve of 'Money-Go-Round'. It whirled out piping hot, frothy milk to cover tiny cups of dark, sticky coffee. A foreign gentleman in a corner booth was having an imaginary argument with an invisible foe about damage to the nearside wing of his Austin Cambridge and behind him, a one-armed Irishman fended off a hag selling bunches of lucky heather and she told him his children would be barren whilst he sucked out the innards from a Walnut Whip. I loved it there and ordered more cappuccino, just to sit back and simply take in all that this new theatre could bring.

Interview time. I was in a stuffy, mouldy, musty old office above Blenheim Terrace smack in the middle of the university campus. Below me was the bookshop, and ahead lay my future. It was October, new term time, and outside, through the grubby, cracked window

I saw the pavements crammed with trestle tables set out by the countless banks all jostling for business, all scrabbling to secure accounts opened by freshers with grant cheques burning holes in the pockets of their grandfathers' trenchcoats. From up there the boys looked like countless mini Morrisseys and the girls looked lovely in black leggings and lace. The place had a carnival atmosphere to it; there were banks to the bookshop's left, a trendy stationer's to the right and a wine merchant reclined at the end of the row – I liked the feel of the place a lot.

Around the room pile upon pile of antiquarian books were stacked up high, some piles were covered in dust sheets and some just piled thick with dust. It felt more like a storeroom than the manager's office. Beams of sunshine poured in like searchlights, tracing their way through the breaks in the tattered blinds. I was confident, cool and composed and I crossed my legs and straightened the tassel on my burgundy loafer – that was better; now my interview could begin.

The manager's name was Clive Luhrs and he looked like Mycroft Holmes, Sherlock's elder and cleverer brother. He appeared almost seven feet tall and he didn't look comfortable with it – like he was stretching himself just being him. Almost forty years old, I guessed, and that number pretty much tallied with the amount of hairs left remaining on his gigantic, ostrich egg of a head. I could see his thunderous brain pumping away, like a beating heart held in a tightened fist as he scrutinised each and every word of my CV – it contained more fiction on those two pages than was in the entire bookshop. A ripple of fear passed through me. Oh, God – I was going to be found out. 'Tell me, David, I'm fascinated – how exactly do you pronounce your surname?'

Oh no. I knew all along that it was a mistake applying under Linés. Why, David, couldn't you just be David Lines? Always with the someone else thing – and now look where it got you. I panicked, and for a second I was lost and then I remembered why Paul split The Jam and how he took on a new direction, a different image and how it got him where he was. I took strength from his irony and his self-belief and I straightened my knitted tie, and replied. 'It's pronounced Lin-ay.' I really wasn't expecting that as his opener. Still, I told myself to stay with it.

'Right, and where does that come from?'

'It's of French descent, as I am.'

'I thought so. I like names – mine's of Belgian origin. We seem to be spread quite thinly over here. There's a Luhrs in Lowestoft that I know of, but he will not answer my calls nor will he respond to my letters and the only others I have details for are in Luxembourg and they're next on my list. It says here that you're a trained classical pianist, conversational in Attic Greek and an excellent steeplechaser?'

Idiot boy. 'That's correct.'

'Marvellous – so where do you find the time to fit in the paragliding?'

'Oh, it's not too difficult – I alternate between that and the freshwater mussel diving.'

'Of course, of course. And what are you reading at the moment?'

I'm glad he asked me that. I'd rehearsed the answer. 'My bedside table positively *creaks* at the moment. The poor thing struggles under the weight of Orwell's *Keep The Aspidistra Flying*, *The Collected Socialist Poems Of Hugh MacDiarmid*, Elizabeth David's *An Omelette And A Glass Of Wine*, an enchanting retrospective of the works to date of Helmut Newman whose title temporarily escapes me, *Second From Last In The Sack Race* and then there's *Brideshead Revisited* which I'm revisiting for the second time due to the fact that the first time I visited I couldn't cope with that tiresome teddy bear.'

Luhrs looked absolutely stunned. I must have done it – I'd only gone and pulled it off. 'Aloysius?'

'Bless you.'

He slowly shook his massive head and gestured towards the door. I got up, extended my hand and shook his, stuck my beret on my head and left. I thought I'd impressed – fingers crossed. Looking back, I'd got too close to myself to see it, but without realising it, I'd only gone and turned into a cross between Paul Weller and Quentin Crisp.

It took a whole week for Clive Luhrs to make up his mind. Maybe he thought we were both European brothers in it together, maybe he just didn't have anyone else to fill the position, whatever, but when the phone rang during the break in *Coronation Street*, you could have knocked me down with a feather from one of Jack's prize racing pigeons. That night, Dad disappeared into the Welsh dresser and came out with a bottle of Harvey's Bristol Cream – we opened it in celebration of my stepping out of school and making my way in the world and as we all raised our glasses,

Dad proposed a toast, 'To Davey, let's hope he doesn't mess it up.'

The very next day was to be my last day at school. It was a Thursday, and if I got the correct paperwork dealt with by all the various tutors I could walk out of there and never, ever have to go back. I was almost eighteen, and if everything had gone to plan I'd have been there for another eight months and leaving with A levels, not leaving early without even taking them. But things hadn't just gone to plan – they'd gone much, much better.

Instead of toiling away at something I hated I was going to enter a profession – and get paid for it! I was going to work in a university bookshop and have intellectual conversations with arty students and sexy lecturers and learn about great French writers and save up my wages and buy a scooter and get my jeans tailored just like Paul's and take girls out to dinner and become a real-life working man. I got a kiss from Mum and a handshake from Dad and I set off to school behind Chris and Phil with a skip in my step and hope in my heart like I'd never known before. That feeling, it was amazing – someone wanted me to work for them, to give me money to be around them. I loved the feeling and I wasn't being smug, I was just enjoying being wanted.

What I did know was that I didn't want to make a big thing of it in front of people at school. I didn't want drinks down the Bird and I didn't want a party or a present or even a card. I just wanted to slip quietly away. Not out of any desire to be mysterious and enigmatic, but because to some I'd be seen as a stupid failure. But not in my eyes, no. In my eyes I was about to throw free the shackles of Garforth Comprehensive and dive headlong into the glamorous world of Leeds University and its campus bookshop – and I couldn't wait.

I'd got it all planned, how to get out of school with as little disruption as possible. All that I had to do was to go to Mr Johnson's office and tell him the good news, that I'd been given this amazing opportunity and that I wanted to take it. Then, I had to go to the administration office, get my release form and get him to sign it. Mr Johnson wasn't surprised, in fact he positively encouraged me to take my chance. 'Well, David, if I'm honest with you, it's a hell of a break. There are graduates coming out of Leeds University who'd kill for that job. Go on, take it, get out of here – and good luck.' We shook hands and I went and got my form, took it back and he signed it with a flourish. I cleared out my locker, took down the pictures of The Style Council, put them in my bag and I walked swiftly down the main corridor, down the school steps and out into the bright sunshine. I skipped down the path, ran out onto the freshly mown playing fields and in my head The Style Council's 'Headstart To Happiness' began to play. The sun hit my face as the golden strings struck up. I broke into a sprint and I sang along at the top of my voice until I was out, away over the fields and onto the main road home. I stopped at the fence and looked back, over my shoulder at the school. Without a second glance I lit a Gitanes and set off on my path to a fresh and brave new world.

Rik rang me that night to ask where I was and I told him then that I'd left for good. I saw most of my friends the next night in the Bird and I was bought a few drinks and had my back slapped a few times and I could tell from the phone call that Rik wasn't convinced I was doing the right thing but I didn't care – I *knew* that I was.

15

Walls Come Tumbling Down

What an opening line to a pop song! This excellent, blistering, vibrant single from The Style Council was the first thing that I bought with my first ever wage packet. 'Walls Come Tumbling Down' opens with a soulful organ, almost like a wedding march, and then blaring horns pipe in and Weller sneers down his microphone with his biting lyrics denouncing consumerism and Thatcher and telling us we are all responsible for our own destiny. When I heard it for the first time it was like Paul was giving me his approval for my decision to go my own way, just like he did when he had the almighty balls to split The Jam. Again, Paul spoke to me and me alone.

The second thing that I spent my new money on was a present for Kate. I saw her sister, briefly, on the bus and she told me she was home that weekend and was going to be in the Bird on Friday night. I'd bought her, from work, a copy of a paperback book entitled *An Everyday Guide To Modern Theatre.* If I handed in my receipt at the end of the month I'd get a third of the money it cost me back, which was £3.99. I'd put a lot of thought into which book to buy her, and in my lunch hour I walked up Blenheim Terrace, past the banks with their lemon-coloured stone walls in the white light of the October sun and bought some fancy wrapping paper from the studenty card shop. Inside the book I wrote, in my best handwriting, 'To Kate – of whom these days I see far too little, but whose friendship in times both happy and sad has been a source of never-failing joy.'

That Friday night I spent ages getting ready, I listened to both sides of *Café Bleu* whilst doing my hair and deciding what to wear. I eventually went for white Levi's 501s, black espadrilles, black Fred Perry shirt and my red Harrington jacket. I walked to the pub through the Meadow's estate, past the trim front lawns with the garden sprinklers drifting out watery mists which caught the evening sunshine and threw off moving, mobile, mini rainbows all chimney orange, fiery red and purple and yellow and blue.

In the distance, the good people of Garforth rang out the bells of St Mary's at the back of me, just down from Church Lane. They carried clear and true, high above the cricket pitch and the broad beans in the allotments, over the beck and out across the school playing fields. Each pull of the campanologists' ropes tugged tighter on my heartstrings and I was suddenly touched by the wonder of it all. Garforth could be a right shit-hole at times, but very occasionally it shone bright and full of Yorkshire glory. That night, it managed to deliver.

The pub was packed and it wasn't even half-past eight. Thankfully, my hair had decided to behave itself. I'd got Kate's book inside my jacket and my back pocket had twenty quid in it to see me through the night. I was at the bar with a Pernod and black, fag on the go, and I checked around to see who was in. I felt older that night. I wasn't part of the college crowd any more, I was removed from them. I was a worker – an independent boy about town who could easily paint it red if I liked. But I didn't want to; I was just going to have a few drinks, chat to a few people, give Kate her present and then leave. I was a professional now, and I was going to behave like one.

I downed my drink, got another and then headed for the jukebox. The hum of conversation acted as white noise, but I wanted to hear Weller, I wanted him to give me confidence about giving Kate her book – I don't know exactly why, but I was nervous about doing so. In went twenty pence and out came 'You're The Best Thing' – the perfect choice.

There was a sharp dig in my ribs and I turned around to find Lizzie Marlow at my side. 'Hello, Mr Lines. If you've got a moment, I'd like a little word or two with you . . .'

I knew exactly what the word or two was, so I got us drinks and we moved through into the snug. Walking in there was like stepping inside a lung. The once-white walls dripped with nicotine and the carpet was so sticky from all the ale sloshed on it over the years that walking to our seat was like wading through mires of mud. I was fearful of Lizzie's forthcoming rebuke. 'So, tell me, Liz. How's it all going?'

We sat down and she sparked up a Silk Cut. 'Oh,

you know, not so bad – considering that my writing partner just upped and left me for a new life in a book-shop.'

'I know, and I'm sorry. But look, just because I'm not at the sixth any longer it doesn't mean that we can't still write together. In fact, if anything, it'll be better because there won't be any homework to distract me, and I'll have more material – there's this coffee shop in town that I've been going to where the people are just so colourful, where everyday stuff just takes on new meaning, we'll be inspired – look, why don't I take you there? We could take pads and pens and see what we come up with. What do you think? Come on, it'll be fun.'

Lizzie smiled and rubbed my knee. She looked happier. 'Deal.' And then her eyes widened in abject horror and she shouted at me to duck but I didn't, because I didn't know what she was on about, and a dart bounced off the wire, whistled through the air and landed on top of my head, before dropping into the ashtray.

'Excuse me, Lizzie – I really do need to try and stem this bloodflow . . .'

I came out of the toilets with loo paper stuck to my

wound. Rik was in the corridor with a pint of bitter in one hand and a pint of mild in the other.

'All right, man.'

'All right, Linesy.'

'Yeah, safe.'

He was trying not to sway too much but it wasn't working very well. 'Went to the Miner's with Robin and Baker. It got messy.'

'So I see.' I'd walked away from this crowd so it was inevitable I wouldn't get invited for a while. Still, it hurt. No matter – I'd made a choice to start a new life.

'I'm just having a drink with Lizzie, but I got distracted.'

'Is that something to do with the bog roll wrapped around your head?'

'Yeah, something like that.'

Over his shoulder I could see Kate coming in. 'Look, I'll see you later. There's something I've got to do . . .'

Kate went through to the main bar with Mandy Berry and Jane Dean. She was wearing pinstriped jeans tucked into brown suede pixie boots, a white grandad shirt and a man's waistcoat. She looked like a drama student straight out of central casting.

Deep breath. 'Hello, Kate.'

'Hi, darling! How are you?' She air-kissed me on both cheeks and tossed back her hair. She was perfect; her eyes all sixties eyeshadow, her breasts rising and falling in time with my beating heart. God, she was lovely.

'I'm well, thanks. And student life certainly suits you.'

'God, thanks, angel. How's the sixth?'

'No idea – I've left.'

'What?'

'I've left, I'm working in a university bookshop, at Austick's in Leeds.'

'Fuck – that's amazing! Do you like it?'

'Yeah, it's great, I'm surrounded by thousands of books all day long.'

'That's really . . . good.'

'You bet. Listen, have you got a moment . . . in private?'

She stood on one leg and raised an eyebrow, sucked on her Silk Cut and said, 'Sure. What's up?'

I steered her by her arm, away from her friends and into the doorway of the pub. I unzipped my jacket and took out her present.

'This is for you.'

'What is it?'

'It's a present. For you. Go on, open it.'

She took the slender parcel from me, peeled open the paper and studied the book's cover. She didn't know what to say, so she opened it, flicked through it and found the inscription. Kate read it out loud and smiled at me, shaking her head. 'God, thanks. I don't know what to . . . look, can you give me a moment? I need a minute to myself, if that's all right. God, I mean, I had no . . .'

'Kate, it's just a book, you know. Look, if you want me, I'll be slumped at the bar with my mates. It's really nice to see you, you know.'

She kissed me on my forehead and I slunk back inside. She was lost for words and so was I.

I was trying to talk to Rik about work, but Baker was banging on about how girls with tanned ankles are an easy lay. I wouldn't know, I still hadn't had one – a lay or a tanned ankle, come to think about it. It was nearly closing time and I was ready for home. Suddenly, Kate was at my side. She had my book in one hand and a Campari in the other. 'I think we need to get your head seen to – it's bleeding. Walk me home?' I didn't need asking twice.

* * *

We were in her parents' kitchen, giggling like children, trying not to make too much noise. Kate took two red mugs from the cupboard, spooned coffee into each and flicked the kettle on.

'Sugar?'

'Yes, honey?'

She laughed and her eyes lit up and for a moment, she looked like the little girl on the fridge door. She took a step forward and took my face in her hands. They were soft and warm and smelled of strawberries. She drew me closer, she put her lips to mine, closed her eyes and then, then she kissed me longingly, tenderly on my lips. They tingled with passion, my whole *body* tingled, even my brain tingled and as her tongue snaked inside my mouth I felt as if I'd died and gone to heaven. Kate moaned softly and we kissed, rocking against each other, her hand stroking my face. We both naturally fell back onto the kitchen floor. I slipped my knee between her legs and she pushed against me, circling my knee with herself. Kate ran her nails up and down my back, panting, and I was growing, desperate to feel her. Was this really going to be my first time? With *the* Kate Blyton? She peeled off her shirt to reveal a cream, lace bra containing those spectacular breasts.

She nibbled my ear and then as I kissed her soft, flat stomach she unbuttoned her jeans and groaned as I slipped my fingers inside her knickers to find her hot, wet mound. She licked my chest as I explored between her legs and I could taste the charged atmosphere in the room. I undid my 501s whilst we kissed more passionately and as she gently took me in her hand and sighed in my ear, as if on cue, the telephone on the kitchen wall began to ring.

'Jesus!' Kate scrambled for it and urgently whispered, 'Hello?'

She looked at me in disbelief. She looked horrified. Upstairs, someone was stirring, woken by the phone. The moment was gone. 'Yes, that's right. He's here – with me.' Kate scrambled back into her shirt as we heard a footstep on the stair. 'What on earth possessed him to stay out so late? I couldn't *possibly* say, Mrs Lines. Yes, I'll tell him. Goodnight.' And she slammed the phone down with such force that the thing almost came off the wall.

I just sat there, head in my hands, gently rocking from side to side. 'Oh, God – no.'

'Oh, God – yes. That, David, was your mother . . . and she's woken the whole house up.'

'My mother?'

'Yes. She was worried where you'd got to, called some friend of yours called Bowerstein or something, he said you left the pub with me, she got the number out of the book and told me to remind you that you've got work tomorrow so please go home to bed.'

'I don't suppose we could –'

'No, we most certainly couldn't. Now scurry on home to your mother, there's a good little boy.'

'Oh, fuck, I'm sorry – I don't know what got into her.'

'Well, neither do I. Goodnight.'

I tried to make light of it. 'I know what didn't get into you.'

You utter prat, Lines. It was a line unworthy of the desperate situation and I regretted it as soon as I'd opened my mouth. I couldn't stop myself, it was crass and Kate was undeserving of my glib schoolboy-shit joke.

'Get out. Now.'

'How about tomorrow?'

'I'm busy. Goodbye.'

I walked home, my adolescent bubble of sexual tension seeping out into my underwear.

* * *

Before I went inside, I sat outside on the low garden wall and smoked a last cigarette underneath the amber glow of the street light. I was beyond furious. I was out to work, I was an adult and my mother had just gone and ruined what could have been the best night of my life simply by picking up the fucking telephone. I ground the fag out under my heel and stormed in through the back door. Mum was in the kitchen. She looked nervous. 'There you are at last, finally home. Here, I've made you a nice milky cocoa. You can take that up with you once we've had a little chat, it'll help you sleep.'

I took it from her and poured it straight down the sink. She looked hurt and I didn't care.

'David, there's something I want to talk to you about . . .'

'Goodnight, Mother.'

And then I went to bed. The next day came far too soon. Far, far too soon.

I got home from work to find the house empty, although the back door was unlocked. Inside, I called out, and from upstairs came Dad's voice. 'Up here, lad.' I walked up the stairs and into their room and there he was, sitting on the bed. Dad looked very old and very tired and his grey-blue, watery eyes stared out at me from his face which he wore like a mask.

'Where is everyone?'

'They've gone for a walk round the block. I thought we might need some time alone, together, to have a little talk.'

'If it's about last night, I'm very cross with her. She ruined my evening.'

'Lad, it's not your mother. It's about me.'

'Why, what's up? Are you going to have a go as well?'

'You're not listening, Davey. It's not about you this time, it's about me.'

I didn't understand, and I told him so. He stared at some faraway place out of the window. His eyes filled up and he started to tremble, his hands shook and then his whole body shook and he stood bolt upright off the bed and he fixed me with his bright, moist eyes and they begged me to ask him the question. 'What is it, Dad? Tell me what's wrong.'

He distracted himself by winding up his wristwatch and then he checked it against the alarm clock on the bedside table. It was as if he was seeing how much time he had left. Then Dad looked me in the eye and wrestled with himself to get the words out. 'Two weeks ago I went to hospital and I had a chest X-ray. They found a shadow on my lung.'

From nowhere a giant wrecking ball appeared and smacked me in the face at a thousand miles an hour. The impact threw me against the wall and I waited for it to swing back and hit me again.

'I've had some tests carried out and they are positive. I have lung cancer and there isn't much time.'

It was as if someone had pulled a pin out of a grenade and I waited for the enormous explosion, lost forever in the silence before the blast. I had no words. I don't even know if I understood him correctly. The pause hung in the air and I was still waiting for the grenade to go off at any second, but the seconds, they just kept on ticking and ticking, deafening me. We were both left hanging in suspended animation.

Dad tried to regain some composure and I stood up and held him. I could feel his ribs. We just stood there, holding each other. After a while he said, 'We didn't want to tell you straightaway, thought we'd wait till the tests came back.'

'I understand. When will we tell Chris and Phil?'

'Oh, they know they'd found the shadow. We didn't

want to upset you, what with starting your new job and everything . . .'

I was enraged, blind with fury at being kept from this terrible, evil secret that the whole house had shared without me. I wasn't just cross with Dad, I was boiling with rage with all of them for keeping me out of it. I couldn't bear to see anyone so I told Dad that I needed some time on my own to take it all in. He understood, we hugged again, for ages, we cried together and then I put on my boating blazer and went out to the pub to get well and truly blind fucking hammered.

I didn't go to the Bird, I just wandered aimlessly down Main Street and the first one that I came to was the Gascoigne. My head was a tangled mess of emotions and even though I knew I should be at home with my family I simply could not bring myself to be there. Instead, I stood at the bar and I drank and drank until the pain began to numb. I was vaguely aware of a woman, much, much older than me, in her late thirties, maybe even her early forties. She'd been sitting on her own all evening, occasionally brushing past me as she went back to order more gin from the bar. I'd been aware of her looking my way every now and then and when I looked back at her she'd smile a little, then look away. I ordered another drink and she got up and came and stood next to me.

She looked like a barmaid on her night off, white blouse with a black bra visible through it, short black skirt, stockings, cheap heels and no fingernails, cheap make-up but a warm smile. I asked her if she'd like a drink, she said she'd love one and we drank and smoked together. Her cheap perfume turned me on and I wasn't embarrassed by the bulge in my Levi's. We sat down and she rubbed me with her knee under the table.

It was all very straightforward, she knew what I wanted and I knew what she wanted. She wasn't unattractive, in a tarty sort of a way, and when she asked me if I wanted to go home with her and have a nightcap, I didn't hesitate. I'm not proud of it, but I went home with her to her horrid terrace house and I took her, over the sink in full view of the unwashed pots. It was over in minutes. I never asked her her name. I went home immediately after I'd pulled out of her and felt more alive than I'd ever done. On the way out of the door I saw a copy of The Jam's *Setting Sons* album on top of the stereo. I couldn't believe it. 'You like The Jam?' I asked.

'No,' she said, 'my eldest lad does.'

* * *

Mum and Dad had taken Phil to feed the ducks at Fairburn Ings and Chris and I had offered to do a bit of gardening, nothing special, just a bit of mowing, a spot of tidying up here and there. Breakfast had been the first time I'd seen them all since Dad had broken the news to me and although I was still feeling very much left out, the previous night had distracted me enough to view things through fresh eyes. I had lost my virginity and I felt like a man. The way in which I did it, compared to the way I had almost done it the previous night, was devoid of any romance or love or an ounce of respect. It didn't repulse me at all, even though I thought it would when I woke up. It didn't; if anything it had the opposite effect – it empowered me.

Chris and I hadn't yet spoken about Dad's illness and I was glad that we had the opportunity to talk about it on our own, man to man. We spent the first hour working solidly on the garden with nothing other than a few words about who was hoeing and who was mowing and how much we should lop off the top of the Michaelmas daisies. We took a break and I said I'd make some coffee; when it had brewed I took it out onto the patio along with a Penguin biscuit each. 'The garden looks good, bro.'

'Yeah, it needed it. We haven't been doing much with it since we found out about Dad. He hasn't felt up to it, you know?'

I could feel my hackles rising and I watched as Chris unwrapped his Penguin and scraped his teeth down through the surface of the chocolate coating, leaving a pair of wobbly grooves like uncertain skis in old, brown snow. I thought for a minute about how it came to be that I'd been left out, kept clear of the family secret, and I asked if there was anything else I should know. Chris swallowed the rest of his biscuit, thought hard and studied his fingernails. They were scraggly from being bitten and he sat on his hands to hide them. He blew air out through his puffed-up cheeks and went on. 'Last night, Dad wanted to go to the bathroom, but he couldn't manage the climb. I had to help haul him up but by the time we'd got to the little landing halfway it was, you know, too late.'

Being presented with such an out of the blue, graphic visual image of a raw secret revealed like that was nothing less than a fist in the forehead for me. I had no idea that Dad couldn't climb stairs – he used to go up them three at a time like a mountain goat just to get me to turn my music down. I didn't know what to say next so I just sat there, swimming around in the sea of stars in front of my eyes, lost in a galaxy of gloom. Eventually, 'I had no idea.'

'No, brother – you have absolutely no idea. Didn't you even notice he'd stopped smoking? Hadn't you heard that fucking cough?'

'I just thought he had a bad cold, that's all.'

'The only thing you'd notice around here is if we'd run out of shampoo and your hairdryer had blown a fuse.'

'That's far from fair.'

'Maybe, but it's bang on the nail. No, David, you have no idea because you're so wrapped up in your own little Weller World. You didn't see it, and to be truthful you don't see anything. We only kept it from you till we were sure what it was because it made it easier on us. He begins chemotherapy next week and he's terrified all his hair will fall out.'

I was being shut out, information was being kept from me by my own family. What was I all of a sudden – the enemy? 'Why the fuck didn't you tell me that Dad was so bad?' A fat tear sploshed down onto my khaki desert boot and I was grateful for that last spray of Scotchguard. The thought wasn't lost on me that whilst Chris was chastising me for being so selfish and overly dramatic, I was thinking about footwear.

'Because you'd just have gone and made it seem so much worse.'

Where the hell did that come from? 'Chris, man, how could I have possibly made things worse? What in the name of sweet Jesus are you talking about?'

I'd got an idea where the conversation was going, and from there, it looked like it was heading for a fight.

'By just being you! You're such a sodding great drama queen, the last thing that this house needed was to be deluged with non-stop deliveries of baskets of exotic fruit and endless bouquets of stupid flowers dripping in sentimental "Get Well Soon" cards. You are the master of the grand gesture and, frankly, we didn't need it then and we don't need it now. What we do need, is calm – and you just don't *do* calm . . .'

I got the feeling that there might be more where that came from, but for the moment that was it. For a second I felt incredibly small. 'Cheers.'

'Don't mention it. What shall we do now?'

'Let's get the shears on that cottoneaster. The thing's out of control – before we know it, it'll have taken over the entire garden and it'll be eating its way into next door's. Then there'll be trouble . . .'

'Whatever you say. Shall I get the stepladder?'

'Yeah, but hold on a minute – I've got an idea . . .'

Ten minutes later we were up in the family bathroom, standing next to each other in front of the mirror. We looked back at our reflections; Chris's face was like a startled rabbit staring at me in abject horror at what was about to happen. He could not escape even if he wanted to, such was the fear which froze him to the lino. I raised my right hand and into view in the mirror came the cut-throat razor, the blade shimmering a twinkly silver.

I gently placed the salmon pink hand towel around my brother's shoulders, motioned to him to sit down on the side of the bath and he did so, entirely at my mercy and compliant to the last. I could feel the fear through the towel. His words took their first, faltering steps from his lips, wary of what they might bump into. 'Why are you doing this to me?'

'I told you, it's a show of strength from us to Dad. It's to show him that we're with him all the way, right the way through this. If his hair's going to fall out with chemotherapy then we'll all go bald, too. Now, put your head down, there's a good lad.' I raised the razor to the top of his head and the words bounced off the bathroom mirror, ricocheted right back and slapped me hard in the face. I looked up, and there was my father. Christ, I even sounded like him. 'Now, put your head down, there's a good lad . . .' I didn't know who was the more scared – Chris for being confronted with a big brother gone mad, or me for almost butchering my brother. I tried to brush it off, make light of it. 'Mate, it's a stupid idea! You're right. Tell you what, you nip downstairs and stick the kettle on and I'll be down in a sec after I've had a quick pee.' Chris walked, trembling and shaking, out onto the landing. He was in shock and so was I. Was I really going to go through with it and scalp him?

I stared at my face and my father stared back at me and I pushed my face right up to the mirror, so close that my breath steamed it up. 'Are you in there, Dad?' There was no answer and so I asked of my reflection one more time, 'Dad, are you in there? Am I turning into you?' Again there was no answer, but downstairs the back door slammed shut and I could hear my poor brother running away from me down the garden path, making good his escape.

I made some tea in a pot, not a mug, in case Chris came back. The chances of that happening were always slim given that his elder brother had just succeeded in delivering a very passable performance of a grade A schizophrenic. Or maybe it wasn't a performance, I didn't know any more. My head was so full of strangers tramping around inside it that just trying to grab hold of an even vaguely unhysterical thought was like jostling my way through an angry crowd. I could hear them upstairs, the strangers in my head, clicking their heels on the floorboards of my mind.

I listened to some Jam. I played the old 'Funeral Pyre' single. The sleeve illustration is of Munch's *The Scream* – it is haunting, chilling, stark and barren, like something that Death doodled whilst killing time. The B-side's equally, if not more mortifying. It's a cover of an old Who song, 'Disguises'. I was so sick of disguises – I needed to get back to the real me. I finished my tea and got on my bike and cycled down to the barber's in Main Street. It was empty and shabby and wasn't fit to kneel in the shadow of Grampa Lines's old barber's shop. It was missing even the fundamental basics of a barber's – there wasn't a *Titbits* or a *National Geographic* to be found for love nor money. I slid into the chair (not pneumatic) and the fat, ruddy pig of a barber appeared. 'Afternoon, sir. What would you like?'

I looked at my perfectly cropped cut, identical in every way to Paul Weller's, just like it had been for years. I took my time, admired it from every angle then finally I said, 'Clippers. Grade one. Shave the lot off.'

16

A Man Of Great Promise

It appears that some time around the time that Paul Weller decided to split The Jam, he did so under the cloud of death. Paul had been on holiday in Italy and returned to find the black news of the demise of his old school friend and early member of The Jam, Dave Waller. Dave had been at Shearwater County Secondary School with Paul and joined The Jam roughly twelve months after the band first got together. From what I can gather, Dave wasn't particularly musical, but what he did do was introduce Paul to literature, and Paul wrote this Style Council song, 'A Man Of Great

Promise', as a tribute to his late friend. For me, it was the standout track on The Style Council's album *Our Favourite Shop*, and it helped me in no small measure to deal with what Dad was going through. It's classic Weller, and opens with church bells, not what you'd think given the subject matter, there's no clanging bell of doom – instead, the bells are like those you'd hear at a wedding, full of celebration. That's what this is, it's a celebration of a man's life. It's funky and upbeat and light and soulful and the piano tinkles and the bass pumps and Paul sings high and breezily – it's a song full of colour and warmth. It was exactly what I needed to help guide me through those dark and desperate days. 'A Man Of Great Promise' was the light in the distance, the distant beacon blinking on the shore for me.

The change in Dad was dramatic and instantaneous. Almost overnight he went from his old self to an old man and we could not kid ourselves that this was just some blip, something which would quietly go away. Cancer's not the sort of thing you can sweep under the carpet.

Three days later we were about to take my father to the hospital to begin his course of chemotherapy. He sat downstairs on the sofa whilst me and Mum sat on my bed and talked together. 'What will they do to Dad?'

'They'll give him some pills to try and make him better. Your father won't like them, they'll make him feel sick and then his hair will fall out.'

'Just like that?'

'No, not just like that, but over the next few weeks it'll come out in clumps and he'll also get very fat.'

Big tears welled up in Mum's eyes and she tipped back her head to stop her mascara from running. I took her thin hand and held it in mine. I could feel the pulse in her wrist and I stroked her face and she dabbed at her eyes with a tissue and then she stroked my hand back. We were in our best clothes. We hadn't talked about it, we just both felt like dressing up – it was the sort of day that required best clothes, like armour. Mum was in a two-piece navy suit with court shoes to match and under her jacket she wore a cream blouse and a cameo brooch on her lapel. I wore my heart on my sleeve and started crying. 'Will they make him better?'

'They'll do their best, love.'

'Will he die today?'

'Not today, David. But soon. You have to prepare yourself. We all do.'

'I've made Dad a tape to listen to whilst he's having his treatment.'

'That's nice, dear.'

'It's some of my favourite songs. Do you think he'll like it?'

She smiled and shook her head. 'No.'

Dad was very quiet in the taxi on the way to the hospital. He didn't drive because they'd told us that they were unsure how his body would respond to the treatment and that he might have to stay overnight but they wouldn't know till after the first dose had been administered. Chris and Phil were at school and I'd swapped my rota day off to go with Mum and Dad. I wanted to know as much as I could about what they were going to do to him. I'd made a list of questions that I wanted to ask the consultant, and I added another one about why he was going to get fat. The taxi pulled up outside the hospital and outside, on the steps, a group of nurses stood around, smoking. Next to them was a man in a wheelchair, his arm hooked up to a drip. He was wearing blue and white striped pyjamas and he was also smoking, although he smoked his cigarette through the hole which had been cut in his neck.

Dad looked scared whilst we spoke to the consultant. He hardly said a word and sat very still, just nodding whilst they answered my questions. The getting fat thing was due to steroids, apparently. I gave him a kiss and a hug and he looked up at me and stared into my eyes and began blinking like mad. I thought he was sending me a message in Morse but he wasn't, he was just trying not to cry in front of his firstborn, his eldest son.

A young nurse arrived with a wheelchair and my father walked towards it like a man going to the guillotine. Mum whispered something in his ear and he managed a faint smile, sat down in the chair and was quietly wheeled away. I asked the consultant if I could speak to him some more and he looked at his watch and said that that would be fine, but just for a minute. A minute was all that I needed – I had an idea and I needed to put it to him. 'Tell me how bad the cancer is.'

The consultant frowned and looked at his watch again. I took that as a bad sign. 'I think that it's fair to say that the malignancy is at a rather advanced stage.

Look, cancer is never good, it is, by its very nature, a bad thing. There are just differing degrees of bad. There's bad, very bad and really very bad.'

'So just how bad is it?'

'It's not good, let's put it like that.'

'It's just one lung?'

'No, I'm sorry to say that both lungs are affected.'

'What if it were only one lung?'

'Then if the other lung were entirely free, we could possibly remove the infected lung and see what happened.'

'And Dad could survive with one lung?'

'It's not unheard of.'

'Then take them both out and give him one of mine.'

The consultant didn't know where to look or what to say. I was being completely sincere and genuine and to me it was the only logical solution: my father needed a lung and I had one going spare – simple as that. The consultant looked away, and then back at me. 'That's a very good idea, but it's simply not possible, I'm afraid.'

'Why not?'

My questioning was making him uncomfortable and it was making me uncomfortable not getting a straight answer. 'Seriously, it's a proper offer. I'm sure my lungs are fine – I've only been smoking for five years.'

'And how old are you now?'

'I'm eighteen.'

'So don't you think you should think about stopping smoking yourself?'

'Absolutely.'

'Good. And once again, thanks very much but let's just see how well your dad responds to the treatment before we go and harvest your organs, shall we?'

'OK – but it's there if we need it.'

'Deal.'

I put my hand out to shake his but he went even before he saw it.

Mum went back home on the bus and I said I needed to go into town. I wanted to be alone. I got a cup of coffee from the machine and thought about going outside to have a smoke with the nurses who'd be looking after Dad, then decided not to. I went for a walk in the hospital garden and sat, quietly, for hours on a bench and I thought about life, and about death and how long it would take for my hair to grow back. I desperately wanted to talk to my father, the thought of losing him was way too upsetting so I went back inside and I set out to find him. It wasn't difficult – I just asked a nurse and she took me straight to him, to a ward where he lay fast asleep, curled up, recovering from his treatment. I didn't wake him.

17

The Cost Of Loving

Immediately after the death of my father I turned into a magpie. My mother invited me inside his wardrobe, to see what would fit, what would be fitting for me to have. I wore his black tie to his funeral. I wore his watch, and every time I stared at its face, his stared back at mine. I fell upon his Aquascutum raincoat and collection of Double Two shirts with relish, his leather gloves, his leather wallet all found their way into my possession. His drawer in the dressing table contained five different lighters. My wardrobe became a little shrine. Mum and I counted his ties: there were 122 of them. Combs took on an even greater meaning for me, and cabinets were searched for secrets. Tie clips and cufflinks, signet rings, nail files, army ID chain, photographs of his parents: these were the prizes, the personal mementos of my old man. I did not feel like a robber of graves, more like an archivist.

Leather-bound pocket diaries which dated back years suddenly became completely fascinating; I devoured insignificant dates filled with entries like 'collect dry-cleaning' and for a while became obsessed with unearthing the full story of 'Menai Straits: 1.30 pm'.

I read them all, looking for something; a clue, maybe? And to what? No, I told myself, I was just being nosey. Peeping through the curtains of the pages of a man's life. It was mainly business stuff – names, appointments, figures. But all captivating to me, nevertheless. I didn't listen to much music at this time, but I did play 'The Cost Of Loving' a great deal. I hummed it to myself all the time; 'doo-dut dut-dut-derr, doo-dut dut-dut-derr' – it was like my mantra, it went some way in keeping me calm.

I helped Mum choose the casket from the man from

the Co-Op. He came round with a catalogue and showed us about as much compassion as if we were ordering a new double mattress. He flicked through the various pages with a look of complete boredom on his face, even looking away as he spoke to us, 'You can have this in oak or pine. The handles stay the same, though . . .'

The vicar came to the house and asked questions about my father so that he could stand in front of our family and friends and sound like he knew him. The answer to 'What were his hobbies?' – 'Fishing . . .' – became 'Bill was an avid angler, well known for spending hours on all fours, stalking double-figure grass carp . . .' The vicar had never set eyes on my father.

On the day that my father was cremated we all had funeral hair. It was flat. Outside, it was blustery and the September sunshine was broken. We all were. At half-past one, the man from the Co-Op came with his colleagues and opened the door of the funeral car for my mother. She climbed inside and we followed her, not one of us taking our eyes off the hearse in front that contained the coffin. When I first set eyes on it, that was when the word was driven home most; dead.

I was expecting something larger, something bigger than the coffin – something more . . . stately. And then I thought that that's all the casket is, really; clothes for the dead.

The drive to the crematorium was an easy one; the traffic was light and the journey was smooth. 'Your dad would have loved a ride in this,' said my mum.

I looked at Chris and at Phil and thought how grown-up he appeared. He caught me studying him and looked at me and said, 'What will become of us?'

'We'll be all right,' said Mum.

'Do you think there'll be many people there to see Dad off?' I asked.

'We'll have to see,' said Mum.

The Co-Op had sent four pallbearers, each in cheap, black nylon suits which did not fit. Either the trousers were too long in the leg or their waistbands were far too tight. It was not fitting for a man whose life had been made to measure. They slid the coffin out of the car and then lifted it up onto their shoulders and carried my dad inside. Mum and I and Chris and Phil followed him, and them, inside. I was struck by how cold it was inside a crematorium. I thought it would have been much hotter. As we walked in, I looked up, for just a moment, and was brought to my senses by the sea of faces; I was expecting a rivulet – not an ocean. 'Doo-dut dut-dut-derr, doo-dut dut dut-derr . . .' Paul's mantra helped me to keep calm.

We sat down and I was instantly aware of the weight of the congregation which was seated behind me. It felt as if it was surging against my shoulders, almost moving me towards the Co-Op coffin. I decided there and then that I would prefer to be buried; I'd much prefer to lay beneath the cold earth than go up in flames. I resigned myself to the fact that my father was going out in one glorious blaze and turned to face the vicar.

He spoke about my father as if they had been best friends since junior school and with a warmth and sincerity like that of a brother. He talked of my dad as if they had been through heaven and hell together and at the end of his address we should have been up on our feet and throwing flowers at him as if we were at the RSC. It was a virtuoso performance – the two men had never even met. The sepia rinse of memory washed over me and I wondered if the vicar had originally thought of a life treading the boards. He'd have made a perfect Hamlet. When he made the improvised move of winking at me when he said my name in his sermon, I simply gaped back; my mouth wide open like a wound.

Once the last prayers were dealt with we watched the coffin on the conveyor belt as it slid slowly behind the curtains to the taped music which came out of only one of the two speakers. The vicar nodded and we stood up and filed outside, back into the cars and were driven back to the house where we having the wake.

We had made sandwiches; ham, cheese, ham and cheese, ham and tomato, cheese and tomato, cheese and pickle. There was potted meat in white and potted meat in brown. And Twiglets. We had made mushroom vol-au-vents and there were sticks of celery in a vase, all of this laid out on the dining-room table over which we had laid a large, crisp white tablecloth. There were two bottles of sherry and I was in charge of keeping people topped up with either tea, coffee or the Bristol Cream. As I did so, moving from guest to guest, I thought about how much longer any of us there were going to be around for. I liked to think about Dad being with Granny and Grampa Lines, up above us in the great hairdresser's in the sky.

I met cousins of my mum's who I never knew existed.

People who I'd never even heard of came to the funeral and I was shocked at how much I wanted to know about them: 'You're my mum's second cousin, right? So what does that make us? And you've got two daughters, so what does that make them and me?' I wanted to discover them all. I liked being surprised by relatives who I'd never met before; I liked the sense of belonging to something much bigger.

I was sorry to see them go, and we promised to keep in touch when we said our goodbyes: 'It's been lovely meeting you. I do hope to see you again soon.' Soon? I'd never set eyes on some of these people. I really did hope to see them again. It felt like the waste of a family, being part of something, something so thick and binding like blood and then never seeing them again. It felt like a terrible, terrible waste. When would I see them again? At their funeral? At mine? At some distant and unimaginable point in the future – when I get married? When my first child is christened? When somebody else here dies? 'Goodbye. Drive home carefully. We should maybe do this again . . .'

We all helped clear up together. We washed the cups and saucers and collected up cocktail sticks. The house was so quiet, so eerie. I ran the Hoover round just to make some background noise. We all sat down and had a cup of tea. 'There,' said Mum. 'That's that, then.'

I went to my bedroom, lay on my bed and thought about my father. I thought about his love of Heinz salad cream and how the taste of it makes me gag. I thought about how beetroot was his favourite food and how if it came within six feet of me I'd try and run a mile. Smiling to myself, my head on my pillow, I remembered tiny things that seemed insignificant until that day. They became important to hang on to. I thought about sledging in the snow on Christmas Day. I don't know how old I could have been, four, five? I got a sledge as my present. A beautiful wooden sledge with iron runners and oval handles on either side. Dad and I dragged it up to the top of the hill, to the top of Selby Road and there, against the backdrop of the big houses set behind their huge iron gates in the soft, floating snow I looked into his eyes, like milk in water, and said 'Thanks, Dad. This is just perfect.'

'Isn't it, lad. I made it snow just for you, Davey. Just for you . . .' He picked me up and plonked me on the back of the sledge and sat down in front of me. I wrapped my arms around his waist and held on as tight as I could. The snow must have been six inches deep and slowly the sledge began to edge down the hill before it picked up speed and we hurtled to the bottom, screaming and laughing all the way.

I thought about all the times he told me to turn my music down. 'For God's sake – will you just turn that bugger off for ten minutes!' But he wasn't there to tell me any more. I turned on my stereo and dropped the needle onto the record. I turned the volume up to ten on the dial – something unheard of when Dad was in the house – and then I took the record off. It didn't seem the same any more.

18

It's A Very Deep Sea

In the weeks following the death of my father, I was gripped by a strange new urge. My mission in life was to mend things. Anything that needed mending, I was the man for the job. If a shelf so much as looked as if it was wonky, out would come the screwdriver. Mowing the lawn was a weekly must-do and I became almost obsessed with painting the skirting boards throughout the house.

Chris and Phil were slowly getting used to Dad not being around and Mum started taking driving lessons. We were getting it back together, albeit slowly, but we were building a new life; one without Bill Lines.

I played The Style Council's 'It's A Very Deep Sea' constantly. I must have listened to this track twenty or thirty times a day. Minimum. It starts with a swishing cymbal and a piano intro which reminds me of the intro to Gloria Gaynor's 'I Will Survive' and then it sort of just *drifts* for a while. I feel like I'm drifting when I play it. Even when I play it today it evokes the feeling of loss that I felt. I was all at sea for months, and 'It's A Very Deep Sea' acted as an anchor for me, it stopped me from feeling adrift. It is one of the finest pieces of work, in my humble opinion, that Paul Weller has ever produced. Musically, it is utterly brilliant; melancholy, thoughtful, atmospheric. It makes me feel like I'm floating out in the middle of an ocean. At the time I felt like an island of loss surrounded by a sea of grief. The song rises and falls, like water moving. It ebbs and flows and laps at my feet and carries me with its momentum. Towards the last section there is a real feeling of crescendo and DC Lee's honeyed tones join with Paul's as the record turns, like tide, and gently slips away as if singing someone to sleep. It sounded to me like the sound of someone drowning. At the end of the track the cymbal swishes back in and gulls call; I picture them hovering above cliff tops with the deep sea below.

I was enjoying working at the bookshop. I wasn't screwing up and, although at first I felt daunted at being surrounded by graduates, the feeling slowly subsided and I soon came to use it as a focus for me, something to concentrate on. And I read. Oh, did I read. I read a book on the bus to work, I read a book in the shop if I ever got a moment, I read a book in my lunch break and then again on the bus on the way home. When I wasn't reading a book, I was reading about books in *The Bookseller*.

I worked with nice people, good people. Most of them had been to university, though not all. I really liked Douglas Picken who ran the basement. This department was social sciences and included subjects like women's studies, politics, history and philosophy. Doug was in his early fifties and drank a bottle of sherry every night. He had a lifelong love affair with jazz and had an encyclopedic knowedge of the subject. In his youth he'd played the cornet with Humphrey Lyttleton. We talked about jazz for hours: 'Back in those days, Dave, you'd be playing three or four different gigs a night. Maybe a pub first, then onto a dance somewhere and then onto a club. Great days – pissed senseless at the end of every night . . .' He had a wind-up gramophone underneath his desk and would play me some of his favourites; Bix Beiderbeck was his hero and we'd often spend afternoons doing stock checks whilst Bix blared out. I took him a copy of 'Have You Ever Had It Blue' by The Style Council because it has a fabulous jazzy feel to it and I thought that he'd enjoy hearing it: 'Right, Dave – let's see what these funny-looking buggers sound like . . .' He wasn't impressed: 'Sodding amateurs.' I didn't mind, he was a different generation and I liked having a friendship with a much older person. It was something new to me.

Mum had decided that she wanted to move. 'There's a ghost in this house,' she said. 'The ghost of your father – and it's a ghost I can well do without.' We started looking through the property press each week. Not feverishly, but with an eye open for something appropriate. 'It's just the upheaval of it all, David. I like the idea of moving away, and each day I like it more and more – it's just the thought of things like tea chests and packing cases – it's all a bit . . . overwhelming.'

'I know what you mean. But we've all got to move on in our own ways, but together and at the same time.'

Mum nodded. 'I think I'll get my driving lessons out of the way before we look to move. I think the house will sell best in the summer when the garden's at its best. And we're not overlooked out there, which is a bonus.'

'Mum,' I said. 'You'll never be overlooked.'

Chris, Phil and I watched Mum pull up outside the kitchen window at the wheel of her driving instructor's Mini Metro. 'He's a wrestler at the weekends,' said Phil. Mum chatted for a couple of minutes, got out of the car and then sprang over the low garden wall and skipped through the back door into the kitchen.

'How's it going?' asked Chris.

'It's going very nicely, thank you. So well, in fact, that Mike's putting me in for my test.'

'Bugger me,' I said.

'I know,' said Mum. 'That's what I thought.'

Rik went to university. When he passed his A levels the year before, his parents gave him their Mini Metro as a gift. I was thrilled for him; he'd got a place at Birmingham to do a degree in brewing. There were only a very small number of people accepted onto a very select course each year. 'One day,' he told me, 'I'm going to have my own brewery.' I didn't doubt him for a single moment. We kept in touch. Sort of. I went and stayed with him for a weekend once, travelling down on a National Express coach. It was nice to see Rik, but I could tell almost straightaway that student life wasn't for me. I suspected as much from what I'd seen from working at the university bookshop, but spending time there confirmed my suspicions. I met some really lovely people that weekend, but it only takes one bad apple and a particularly stuck-up girl spoiled – for me – Bowerman's barrel. 'What do you do?' she asked.

'I work in a bookshop.'

'Oh, how interesting,' she said, 'and what do you want to do when you grow up?'

I didn't visit again.

My own university was the Austick's University Bookshop in Leeds. I was learning so much about life, people, the arts; it felt as if I was living a dream. My brother Chris was very focused about what he wanted to do, and he'd set his heart on going to art college to train to become a designer. I knew he'd be brilliant.

Phil was cracking on with his school studies and Mum and the three of us let our lives steady themselves, letting each new day help us find the right balance between a life with Dad and a new life without him. We could make it if we stuck together. I knew that. We all did.

I had some unfinished business which I needed to deal with and I'd made a phone call to set up a meeting earlier in the week. Thankfully, she'd agreed to meet me.

It was a Saturday in late November and I was nervous about seeing her. The early, organised Christmas shoppers were muffled against the early morning bite as it blew down Briggate in the centre of Leeds. I quickened my pace at the thought of frothy coffee. I was early, and by the time I'd ordered, she was late. I looked out of the café window and watched women weighed down by bags from Woolworth's.

It was an entirely different crowd of people in the Andromeda that Saturday. None of the usual faces who I'd got used to seeing each morning before work were there, it was just people who were taking a break from shopping. I sat down, and after a moment wiped away the steam from inside the window with a serviette, revealing my reflection in the glass. I lit a cigarette and sipped my coffee and sat and stared at my face, framed by the steam. I thought about how it was me I was looking at, and not my father or Paul Weller looking back. It was just me. I thought about just how much I will always miss my dad, but that it was a feeling I could live with, and that the heavy veil of grief had begun to lift and thin. I thought about Paul Weller and how I'd always love his music and hold dear all of the things it had taught me, but that all of a sudden Weller's work seemed like a soundtrack to my life, not a blueprint for it. I breathed on the glass and my reflection slowly disappeared before my eyes.

After another ten minutes had passed she finally walked through the door. She looked great, with her hair tied back and she was all snuggled into a huge black winter coat. I stood up and we kissed each other on the cheek and I helped her off with her coat. 'I'll get some coffee.'

'Great. I'll sit here and try to defrost my fingers.'

She sat down and I quickly admired her tight-fitting mauve lambswool sweater as I came back with the drinks.

'It's lovely to see you.' She reached over and touched my hand.

'Thanks, Lizzie. It's lovely to see you, too.'

She smiled a wry smile. 'Right, David. Get your pad and pen out – we've got some writing to do. And one more thing?'

'What?'

'Just for one single moment, would you please stop staring at my breasts.'